Modern Critical Interpretations

Virginia Woolf's To the Lighthouse

Modern Critical Interpretations

Virginia Woolf's

To the Lighthouse

Edited and with an introduction by

Harold Bloom
Sterling Professor of the Humanities
Yale University

Chelsea House Publishers ◊ 1988

NEW YORK ◊ NEW HAVEN ◊ PHILADELPHIA

345 Whitney Avenue, New Haven, CT 06511
95 Madison Avenue, New York, NY 10016
5068B West Chester Pike, Edgemont, PA 19028

Printed and bound in the United States of America

10 9 8 7 6 5 4 3 2 1

∞ The paper used in this publication meets the minimum requirements of the American National Standard for Permanence of Paper for Printed Library Materials, Z39.48-1984.

Library of Congress Cataloging-in-Publication Data
Virginia Woolf's To the lighthouse.
(Modern critical interpretations)
Bibliography: p.
Includes index.
1. Woolf, Virginia, 1882–1941. To the lighthouse.
I. Bloom, Harold. II. Series.
PR6045.072T6867 1988 823′.912 87-23915
ISBN 1-55546-034-8 (alk. paper)

Contents

Editor's Note

This book gathers together a representative selection of the best critical interpretations of Virginia Woolf's novel, *To the Lighthouse*. The critical essays are reprinted here in the chronological order of their original publication. I am grateful to Christina Büchmann for her erudite aid in editing this volume.

My introduction centers upon the relationship between Walter Pater's secularized epiphanies and privileged moments, and those of Woolf, particularly in *Mrs. Dalloway* and *To the Lighthouse*. Hermione Lee begins the chronological sequence of criticism with a study of "completed forms" in *To the Lighthouse*, forms that she sees as Woolf's only answers to death and chaos.

In Jane Lilienfeld's reading, *To the Lighthouse* represents Woolf's mature resolution to her ambivalences towards her parents, particularly towards her mother, while Martin Corner emphasizes instead Woolf's "atheistic mysticism" in the novel.

John Burt, juxtaposing *A Room of One's Own* and *To the Lighthouse*, subtly concludes that Woolf's novel returns despite itself to realism and conventional social order, yet remains a work mourning its own inability to transcend both aesthetic and societal formalisms. A related reading by Gillian Beer establishes *To the Lighthouse* as an elegiac work, by way of a Humean account of experience.

Frank Gloversmith invokes the Bloomsbury aesthetic doctrine of "significant form" as context for *To the Lighthouse*, after which a panel discussion by Gillian Beer, Bernard Bergonzi, John Harvey, and the novelist Iris Murdoch culminates in Murdoch's strong declaration that there is only human experience, rather than a specifically female experience, as feminist critics of Woolf tend to insist.

In this book's final essay, Perry Meisel, while granting the elegiac aspect of *To the Lighthouse*, sees the novel as a crucial work that calls into question the myth of literary modernism. Meisel's emphasis takes this volume full circle, back to my introduction's Paterian appreciation of Woolf's ways of representing the privileged moment of sensation and perception.

Introduction

I

In May 1940, less than a year before she drowned herself, Virginia Woolf read a paper to the Worker's Educational Association in Brighton. We know it as the essay entitled "The Leaning Tower," in which the Shelleyan emblem of the lonely tower takes on more of a social than an imaginative meaning. It is no longer the point of survey from which the poet Athanase gazes down in pity at the dark estate of mankind, and so is not an image of contemplative wisdom isolated from the mundane. Instead, it is "the tower of middle-class birth and expensive education," from which the poetic generation of W. H. Auden and Louis MacNeice stare sidelong at society. Woolf does not say so, but we can surmise that she preferred Shelley to Auden, while realizing that she herself dwelt in the leaning tower, unlike Yeats, to whom the lonely tower remained an inevitable metaphor for poetic stance.

It is proper that "The Leaning Tower," as a speculation upon the decline of a Romantic image into belatedness, should concern itself also with the peculiarities of poetic influence:

> Theories then are dangerous things. All the same we must risk making one this afternoon since we are going to discuss modern tendencies. Directly we speak of tendencies or movements we commit ourselves to the belief that there is some force, influence, outer pressure which is strong enough to stamp itself upon a whole group of different writers so that all their writing has a certain common likeness. We must then have a theory as to what this influence is. But let us always remember—influences are infinitely numerous; writers are infinitely sensitive; each writer has a different sensibility. That is why literature is always changing, like the weather, like clouds in the sky. Read a page of Scott; then of Henry James; try to work out the influences that have trans-

> formed the one page into the other. It is beyond our skill. We can only hope therefore to single out the most obvious influences that have formed writers into groups. Yet there are groups. Books descend from books as families descend from families. Some descend from Jane Austen; others from Dickens. They resemble their parents, as human children resemble their parents; yet they differ as children differ, and revolt as children revolt. Perhaps it will be easier to understand living writers as we take a quick look at some of their forebears.

A critic of literary influence learns to be both enchanted and wary when such a passage is encountered. Sensibility is indeed the issue, since without "a different sensibility" no writer truly is a writer. Woolf's sensibility essentially is Paterian, as Perry Meisel accurately demonstrated. She is hardly unique among the great modernist writers in owing much to Pater. That group includes Wilde, Yeats, Wallace Stevens, Hart Crane, as well as Pound and Eliot. Among the novelists, the Paterians, however involuntary, include Scott Fitzgerald, the early Joyce, and in strange ways both Conrad and Lawrence, as well as Woolf. Of all these, Woolf is most authentically Pater's child. Her central tropes, like his, are personality and death, and her ways of representing consciousness are very close to his. The literary ancestor of those curious twin sensibilities—Septimus Smith and Clarissa Dalloway—is Pater's Sebastian Van Storck, except that Woolf relents, and they do not go into Sebastian's "formless and nameless infinite world, quite evenly grey."

Mrs. Dalloway (1925), the fourth of Woolf's nine novels, is her first extraordinary achievement. Perhaps she should have called it *The Hours*, its original working title. To speak of measuring one's time by days or months, rather than years, has urgency, and this urgency increases when the fiction of duration embraces only hours, as *Mrs. Dalloway* does. The novel's peculiar virtue is the enigmatic doubling between Clarissa Dalloway and Septimus Smith, who do not know one another. We are persuaded that the book is not disjointed because Clarissa and Septimus uncannily share what seem a single consciousness, intense and vulnerable, each fearing to be consumed by a fire perpetually about to break forth. Woolf seems to cause Septimus to die instead of Clarissa, almost as though the novel is a single apotropaic gesture on its author's part. One thinks of the death died for Marius by Cornelius in Pater's *Marius the Epicurean*, but that is one friend atoning for another. However unified, does *Mrs. Dalloway* cogently link Clarissa and Septimus?

Clearly the book does, but only through its manipulation of Pater's evasions of the figure or trope of the self as the center of a flux of sensations.

In a book review written when she was only twenty-five, Woolf made a rough statement of the stance towards the self she would take throughout her work-to-come, in the form of a Paterian rhetorical question: "Are we not each in truth the centre of innumerable rays which so strike upon one figure only, and is it not our business to flash them straight and completely back again, and never suffer a single shaft to blunt itself on the far side of us?" Here is Clarissa Dalloway, at the novel's crucial epiphany, not suffering the rays to blunt themselves on the far side of her:

> What business had the Bradshaws to talk of death at her party? A young man had killed himself. And they talked of it at her party—the Bradshaws talked of death. He had killed himself—but how? Always her body went through it first, when she was told, suddenly, of an accident; her dress flamed, her body burnt. He had thrown himself from a window. Up had flashed the ground; through him, blundering, bruising, went the rusty spikes. There he lay with a thud, thud, thud in his brain, and then a suffocation of blackness. So she saw it. But why had he done it? And the Bradshaws talked of it at her party!
>
> She had once thrown a shilling into the Serpentine, never anything more. But he had flung it away. They went on living (she would have to go back; the rooms were still crowded; people kept on coming). They (all day she had been thinking of Bourton, of Peter, of Sally), they would grow old. A thing there was that mattered; a thing, wreathed about with chatter, defaced, obscured in her own life, let drop every day in corruption, lies, chatter. This he had preserved. Death was defiance. Death was an attempt to communicate; people feeling the impossibility of reaching the centre which, mystically, evaded them; closeness drew apart; rapture faded, one was alone. There was an embrace in death.

The evasiveness of the center is defied by the act of suicide, which in Woolf is a communication and not, as it is in Freud, a murder. Earlier, Septimus had been terrified by a "gradual drawing together of everything to one centre before his eyes." The doubling of Clarissa and Septimus implies that there is only a difference in degree, not in kind, between Clarissa's sensibility and the naked consciousness or "madness" of Septimus. Neither needs the encouragement of "Fear no more the heat o' the sun," because each knows that consciousness is isolation and so untruth, and that the right worship of life is to defy that isolation by dying. J. Hillis Miller remarks that: "A novel, for Woolf, is the place of death made visible." It seems to me difficult to defend *Mrs. Dalloway* from moral judgments that call Woolf's stance wholly nihilistic. But then, *Mrs. Dalloway*, remarkable as it is, is truly Woolf's starting-point as a strong writer, and not her conclusion.

II

Critics tend to agree that Woolf's finest novel is *To the Lighthouse* (1927), which is certainly one of the central works of the modern imagination, comparable to Lawrence's *The Rainbow* or Conrad's *Victory*, if not quite of the range of *Women in Love* or *Nostromo*. Perhaps it is the only novel in which Woolf displays all of her gifts at once. Erich Auerbach, in his *Mimesis*, lucidly summing up Woolf's achievement in her book, could be expounding Pater's trope of the privileged moment:

> What takes place here in Virginia Woolf's novel is . . . to put the emphasis on the random occurrence, to exploit it not in the service of a planned continuity of action but in itself. And in the process something new and elemental appeared: nothing less than the wealth of reality and depth of life in every moment to which we surrender ourselves without prejudice. To be sure, what happens in that moment—be it outer or inner processes—concerns in a very personal way the individuals who live in it, but it also (and for that very reason) concerns the elementary things which men in general have in common. It is precisely the random moment which is comparatively independent of the controversial and unstable orders over which men fight and despair; it passes unaffected by them, as daily life. The more it is exploited, the more the elementary things which our lives have in common come to light. The more numerous, varied, and simple the people are who appear as subjects of such random moments, the more effectively must what they have in common shine forth.

The shining forth is precisely Pater's secularization of the epiphany, in which random moments are transformed: "A sudden light transfigures a trivial thing, a weathervane, a windmill, a winnowing flail, the dust in the barn door; a moment—and the thing has vanished, because it was pure effect." Woolf, like Pater sets herself "to realize this situation, to define, in a chill and empty atmosphere, the focus where rays, in themselves pale and impotent, unite and begin to burn." To realize such a situation is to set oneself against the vision of Mr. Ramsay (Woolf's father, the philosopher Leslie Stephen), which expresses itself in the grimly empiricist maxim that: "The very stone one kicks with one's boot will outlast Shakespeare." Against this can be set Lily Briscoe's vision, which concludes the novel:

> Quickly, as if she were recalled by something over there, she turned to her canvas. There it was—her picture. Yes, with all its greens and blues, its lines running up and across, its attempt at something. It would be hung in the attics, she thought; it would be destroyed. But what did that matter? she asked herself, taking up her brush again. She looked at the steps; they were empty; she looked at her canvas; it was blurred. With a sudden intensity, as if she saw it clear for a second, she drew a line there, in the centre. It was done; it was finished. Yes, she thought, laying down her brush in extreme fatigue, I have had my vision.

"An attempt at something" postulates, for Woolf, a center, however evasive. The apotheosis of aesthetic or perceptive principle here is Woolf's beautifully poised and precarious approach to an affirmation of the difficult possiblity of meaning. *The Waves* (1931) is a large-scale equivalent of Lily Briscoe's painting. Bernard, the most comprehensive of the novel's six first-person narrators, ends the book with a restrained exultation, profoundly representative of Woolf's feminization of the Paterian aesthetic stance:

> "Again I see before me the usual street. The canopy of civilisation is burnt out. The sky is dark as polished whale-bone. But there is a kindling in the sky whether of lamplight or of dawn. There is a stir of some sort—sparrows on plain trees somewhere chirping. There is a sense of the break of day. I will not call it dawn. What is dawn in the city to an elderly man standing in the street looking up rather dizzily at the sky? Dawn is some sort of whitening of the sky; some sort of renewal. Another day; another Friday; another twentieth of March, January, or September. Another general awakening. The stars draw back and are extinguished. The bars deepen themselves between the waves. The film of mist thickens on the field. A redness gathers on the roses, even on the pale rose that hangs by the bedroom window. A bird chirps. Cottagers light their early candles. Yes, this is the eternal renewal, the incessant rise and fall and fall and rise again.
>
> "And in me too the wave rises. It swells; it arches its back. I am aware once more of a new desire, something rising beneath

> me like the proud horse whose rider first spurs and then pulls him back. What enemy do we now perceive advancing against us, you whom I ride now, as we stand pawing this stretch of pavement? It is death. Death is the enemy. It is death against whom I ride with my spear couched and my hair flying back like a young man's, like Percival's, when he galloped in India. I strike spurs into my horse. Against you I will fling myself, unvanquished and unyielding, O Death!"
>
> *The waves broke on the shore.*

"Incessant rise and fall and fall and rise again," though ascribed to Bernard, has in it the fine pathos of a recognition of natural harshness that does not come often to a male consciousness. And for all the warlike imagery, the ride against death transcends aggressivity, whether against the self or against others. Pater had insisted that our one choice lies in packing as many pulsations of the artery, or Blakean visions of the poet's work, into our interval as possible. Woolf subtly hints that even Pater succumbs to a male illusion of experiential quantity, rather than to a female recognition of gradations in the quality of possible experience. A male critic might want to murmur, in defense of Pater, that male blindness of the void within experience is very difficult to overcome, and that Pater's exquisite sensibility is hardly male, whatever the accident of his gender.

Between the Acts (1914), Woolf's final novel, can be read as a covert and witty subversion of late Shakespeare, whose romances Woolf attempts to expose as being perhaps more male than universal in some of their implications. Parodying Shakespeare is a dangerous mode; the fat-out farce of Max Beerbohm and Nigel Dennis works more easily than Woolf's allusive deftness, but Woolf is not interested in the crudities of farce. *Between the Acts* is her deferred fulfillment of the polemical program set forth in her marvelous polemic *A Room of One's Own* (1929), which is still the most persuasive of all feminist literary manifestos. To me the most powerful and unnerving stroke in that book is in its trope for the enclosure that men have forced upon women:

> For women have sat indoors all these millions of years, so that by this time the very walls are permeated by their creative force, which has, indeed, so overcharged the capacity of bricks and mortar that it must needs harness itself to pens and brushes and business and politics. But this creative power differs greatly from the creative power of man.

That last assertion is becoming a kind of shibboleth in contemporary feminist literary criticism. Whether George Eliot and Henry James ought to be read as instances of a gender-based difference in creative power is not beyond all critical dispute. Is Dorothea Brooke more clearly the product of a woman's creative power than Isabel Archer would be? Could we necessarily know that Clarissa Harlow ensues from a male imagination? Woolf, at the least, lent her authority to provoking such questions. That authority, earned by novels of the splendor of *To the Lighthouse* and *Between the Acts*, becomes more formidable as the years pass.

To the Lighthouse: Completed Forms

Hermione Lee

> So that is marriage, Lily thought, a man and a woman looking at a girl throwing a ball . . . And suddenly the meaning which, for no reason at all . . . descends on people, making them symbolical, making them representative, came upon them, and made them in the dusk standing, looking, the symbols of marriage, husband and wife. Then, after an instant, the symbolical outline which transcended the real figures sank down again, and they became . . . Mr and Mrs Ramsay watching the children throwing catches.

The passage draws together, as in the curve of the ball, the three centres of this tripartite novel: the Ramsays' family life; the "symbolical outline," which transcends the "real figures"; and Lily's attempt to master both symbol and reality.

Prue and Jasper, throwing catches, are watched by their parents on a September evening before dinner. It is a family party in a shabby house on the Isle of Skye; there are eight children and some guests—Charles Tansley, a young philosopher; Augustus Carmichael, an old college friend of Mr Ramsay's; William Bankes, a widowed botanist; Lily Briscoe, who paints; and Minta Doyle and Paul Rayley, who are falling in love. One of the younger children, James, has just gone to bed, disappointed because the weather (as his father and Charles Tansley have unkindly assured him) will not be good enough to make the long-promised journey to the lighthouse the next day. Two of the older children are still at the beach with Paul and Minta. Mrs

From *The Novels of Virginia Woolf.* © 1977 by Hermione Lee. Methuen & Co. Ltd., 1977.

Ramsay, upset by the conversation about the lighthouse, is worried in case they will be late: the cook has made a *boeuf en daube* which cannot be kept waiting.

These are "real figures," and this is the stuff of a more than usually uneventful family saga. Charles Tansley, ill at ease in the rather snobbish family who don't like his ties, might find a place in Arnold Bennett's *Clayhanger*. James's disappointment could form a part of Hugh Walpole's *Jeremy*. But the scene in which Mr and Mrs Ramsay watch the children throwing catches suggests that the novel reaches beyond its realistic materials. The people are also shapes, and the shapes convey larger meanings than can be contained in the lives of individuals. The point of view from which the scene is described hovers between the personal and the general.

Nevertheless, *To the Lighthouse* is at an important level a dramatic, realistic, ironic story of a family life which was, to a great extent, Virginia Stephen's. "Writing the *Lighthouse* laid them in my mind" she says of her preoccupation with her parents; and Vanessa Bell, best qualified to judge, comments:

> In the first part of the book you have given a portrait of mother which is more like her than anything I could have conceived of as possible. You have made me feel the extraordinary beauty of her character . . . It was like meeting her again with oneself grown up and on equal terms . . . You have given father too I think as clearly, but perhaps . . . that isn't quite so difficult. There is more to catch hold of.

Vanessa herself is part of *To the Lighthouse*, as one of the Stephen children whose lives with their widowed father inspired James's and Cam's relationship with Mr Ramsay in the last part of the novel, and as Lily Briscoe, whose struggle with her art is as much Vanessa's as Virginia Woolf's own: "God! how you'll laugh at the painting bits in the Lighthouse!" Virginia wrote to her.

The marriage of Leslie Stephen and Julia Duckworth seemed to Virginia Woolf to present an archetypal pattern of sexual antitheses. Her portrayal of the Ramsays makes these contrasts so obvious, and is so characteristic of her treatment of the differences between male and female sensibilities, that the grandeur and subtlety of the relationship seems all the more extraordinary. Mrs Ramsay is beautiful, queenly, shortsighted, philanthropic and inventive. Her intimacy with her children nourishes her natural tendency towards fantasy and exaggeration. Like Mrs Hilbery she is associated with poetry, Mr Ramsay (like Mr Hilbery) with prose. Mr Ramsay does not see what is close to him—the flowers, or his own children's beauty. Instead, with "an eye like an eagle's," he seeks for truth. He is awkward and ungainly in company. He is a stickler for facts, and cannot bear exaggeration or imprecision. Their conflict over the weather is a paradigm of the sexual battle: Mrs Ramsay becomes a fountain of fecundity and Mr Ramsay a "beak of brass." The woman's emotional act of giving sympathy paradoxically fertilizes the man, but more in the manner of a mother feeding her child than a lover:

> He wanted . . . to be taken within the circle of life, warmed and soothed, to have his senses restored to him, his barrenness made fertile, and all the rooms of the house made full of life—the drawing-room; behind the drawing-room the kitchen; above the kitchen the bedrooms; and beyond them the nurseries; they must be furnished; they must be filled with life.

But this is not a simple dialectic. Mrs Ramsay is as dependent on Mr Ramsay for comfort and protection. She rests on the hard certainties of the masculine world "as a child." It is she who is the more pessimistic and who relies on him to turn her thoughts away from doubt and gloom. And, in spite of their contrasted characteristics, they are engaged on the same field of battle, in which they evince similar characteristics of courage and endurance. Mr Ramsay struggles to overcome his sense of failure and transience, Mrs Ramsay brandishes her sword—an image shared by them both—against the "little strip of time"—which threatens her. She attempts to build something that will endure, from social and domestic materials.

Both are trying to come to terms with the fact of death; but there is a difference in the way their attempts are treated. Mr Ramsay is very largely a comic character. His bawling "Best and brightest, come away!" at Miss Giddings, like a character out of Lewis Carroll, his fury at Augustus Carmichael's asking for another plate of soup, his delight when Lily praises his boots, his pose of desolation on the boat, all emphasize the ludicrous side of Leslie Stephen which is summed up by the story

> that he was heard one night slowly ascending the stairs, groaning at each step and loudly exclaiming: "Why won't my whiskers grow? Why won't my whiskers grow?"

The language associated with Mr Ramsay's thoughts frequently takes on the extravagant mock-heroic tone which was used in *Mrs. Dalloway* as an instrument of satire:

> His own children . . . sprung from his loins, should be aware from childhood that life is difficult; facts uncompromising; and the passage to that fabled land where our brightest hopes are

> extinguished, our frail barks founder in darkness (here Mr Ramsay would straighten his back and narrow his little blue eyes upon the horizon), one that needs, above all, courage, truth and the power to endure.

The metaphor of a dangerous expedition also colours the passage in which he is trying to "reach R." Though it is a satirical image imposed from the outside in order to make Mr Ramsay's heroic struggle seem absurd, it is also part of his train of thought; again the mental image is turned into a physical action:

> When the search party comes they will find him dead at his post, the fine figure of a soldier. Mr Ramsay squared his shoulders and stood very upright by the urn.

Mr Ramsay thus participates in the imagery which is used to satirize him. The same is true of the description of his mental processes as the struggle to "reach R," in part an ironical shorthand used by the narrator, but also Mr Ramsay's own method of summing up the extent of his achievement as a philosopher. The subtlety with which the figures of speech hover between the inside and the outside of Mr Ramsay's mind makes it difficult for us to find him altogether comic. At the same time, it is evident that Virginia Woolf did mean Mr Ramsay to be ludicrous, from the way in which she has extrapolated him from Leslie Stephen. Her father was an excellent mountaineer, identified by Thomas Hardy with the Shreckhorn which Stephen (as "gaunt and difficult" as the mountain) was the first to climb. He was also a great walker until late on in life, leading the arduous "Sunday tramps" for fifteen years. But Mr Ramsay's idea of himself as the leader of an expedition is an unreal self-dramatization, and his desire to "be off for a day's walk" "with nothing but a biscuit in his pocket" is felt by Mrs Ramsay to be negligible, mere nostalgia for his youth. The real expedition he leads to the lighthouse is not a strenuous adventure; his children feel the falsity of his identifying on the boat with the brave, simple fishermen. Virginia Woolf has transformed Leslie Stephen's genuine attributes of physical daring and stamina into facets of Mr Ramsay's emotional self-indulgence.

There is no comparable ridicule of Mrs Ramsay's courage and endurance. Nevertheless, an equivalent satirical tone is associated with her which suggests that, like Clarissa, she is not inviolate from criticism. The tone is grandiose, affected, and full of second-rate literary clichés:

> There was something in this of the essence of beauty which called out the manliness in their girlish hearts.

> Had she not in her veins the blood of that very noble, if slightly mythical, Italian house, whose daughters . . . had lisped so charmingly, had stormed so wildly, and all her wit and her bearing and her temper came from them.

> Like some queen who, finding her people gathered in the hall, looks down upon them, and descends among them, and acknowledges their tributes silently, and accepts their devotion and their prostration before her . . . she went down.

An association is made between Mrs Ramsay and the kind of sentimental Victorianism which is to be parodied in *Orlando*. And Mrs Ramsay is at one point explicitly identified with Queen Victoria. But there is a rather different ironic tinge to her imaginary words to Lily at the dinner table:

> "I am drowning, my dear, in seas of fire. Unless you apply some balm to the anguish of this hour and say something nice to that young man there, life will run upon the rocks . . . My nerves are taut as fiddle strings."

Sounding here more like Gwendolen Fairfax than Queen Victoria, she is now being satirized not for her Victorianism but for the littleness of her society feelings, as Clarissa is satirized by Peter Walsh. In both women, the compulsion to be loved (whether as wife, mother, hostess or friend) is presented as a weakness. And Mrs Ramsay has other limitations. She is afraid, like the speaker in Hardy's poem, to

> look into my glass
> And view my wasted skin.

She is uninformed (like Mrs Wilcox in *Howards End*), leaving factual knowledge and differences of opinion to the men. She believes fervently and defensively in the essential value for women of marriage and child-bearing. She is deeply inhibited in her emotional life and, at the same time, interfering and even malicious in her dealings with the lives of others.

The evidence about the Ramsays is constantly reshuffled through the attitudes of different onlookers. Mr Carmichael shows up Mrs Ramsay's desire to be liked by not liking her; Mr Bankes exposes Mr Ramsay's egotistical concern with his works and fame by his own disinterestedness; Lily is amazed at Mrs Ramsay's misjudgements of people and at her universal recommendation of marriage. The children resent, as well as admire, both their parents; beneath the main current of the book there is another story, to be fully expressed in *The Years*, of the second generation's attempt to escape their nineteenth-century background. And the future that the Ramsays set in motion is also a means of judging them. In the last part of the novel Mrs Ramsay is dead, and so are the two children of brightest promise: Andrew, whom Mr Ramsay had said "would be a better man than he had been," and Prue, whom Mrs Ramsay intended to be "happier than other people's daughters." The Rayleys' marriage, which she arranged, has not been a success; and Lily and William Bankes have not married as she hoped they would. At a realistic level it appears that the Ramsays' marriage was an incompatible union between unsatisfactory characters whose plans for others were all unfulfilled.

If one is thus to deny the value of the "real life" of the Ramsays, the only satisfactory conclusion in the book is an aesthetic one. But to say that their relationship is only triumphant when resolved by Lily as part of her picture is to be false to the complex and powerful balance of the novel, which has two moments of climax, not just one. There is a resolution of conflict between Mr and Mrs Ramsay at the end of part 1 which is weighed against Mr Ramsay's arrival at the lighthouse and Lily's completion of her picture in part 3.

> And what then? For she felt that he was still looking at her, but that his look had changed. He wanted something—wanted the thing she always found so difficult to give him; wanted her to tell him that she loved him. And that, no, she could not do . . . A heartless woman he called her; she never told him that she loved him. But it was not so—it was not so. It was only that she never could say what she felt . . . Getting up she stood at the window with the reddish-brown stocking in her hands, partly to turn away from him, partly because she did not mind looking now, with him watching, at the Lighthouse. For she knew that he had turned his head as she turned; he was watching her. She knew that he was thinking, You are more beautiful than ever. And she felt herself very beautiful . . . Then, knowing that he was watching her, instead of saying anything she turned, holding her stocking, and looked at him. And as she looked at him she began to smile, for though she had not said a word, he knew, of course he knew, that she loved him. He could not deny it. And smiling, she looked out of the window and said (thinking to herself, Nothing on earth can equal this happiness)—
>
> "Yes, you were right. It's going to be wet tomorrow." She

> had not said it, but he knew it. And she looked at him smiling.
> For she had triumphed again.

The moment is controlled, and described, by Mrs Ramsay; it is the victory of her beauty and intuition over his desire for speech and hard facts. In a sense she is subjugating him to her will; her smile is one of mastery. But her triumph is also achieved by a relinquishing of the will: she admits his monopoly of the truth, and allows that it will be wet the next day. The scene, by its lyrical fluidity (an intensification of the manner of the whole novel) gives the impression that both minds are simultaneously revealed to each other in silence, even though the narrative is really centered in Mrs Ramsay's consciousness. Thus, although she dominates the moment, it creates a moving sense of unification. A reconcilement of considerable grandeur has taken place between temperaments of extreme emotional disparity.

The force of this scene, however, does not arise entirely from our interest in the realistic personal relationship between Mr and Mrs Ramsay. We come to it after the long first part of the novel has established, in a brilliant variety of ways, an elastic interplay between the real and the metaphysical, so that Mr and Mrs Ramsay's marriage by now seems to be a reconciliation between abstract qualities which gives it a more than merely personal importance. The most obvious of the techniques used to achieve this effect is the manipulation of principles, by now a familiar device for expressing the simultaneity of different levels of experience, whose limitation is that it requires an equally refined sensibility of all its characters: "We do not always think of eternity while serving potatoes; sometimes we just think of serving potatoes. Virginia Woolf's characters never do." Furthermore, they are often ironically aware of the dichotomy between their thoughts and their actions: "Raising her eyebrows at the discrepancy—that was what she was thinking, this what she was doing—ladling out soup." The point of this constant emphasis on the disparity between thought and action is not that it should be psychologically convincing. Perhaps not everyone thinks like this; but everyone in this novel must, because the characters are being used in the service of an abstract argument about the difficulty of infusing shapes with sense. The recognizable shapes of daily life are frequently at odds with the sense which underlies them. This is evident in some of the dialogue, which, like the ladling of soup, is often irrelevant to the flow of consciousness behind it, as in the climatic scene between Mr and Mrs Ramsay:

> "They're engaged . . . Paul and Minta."
> "So I guessed."
> [PAUSE]

"How nice it would be to marry a man with a wash-leather bag for his watch."
[PAUSE]
"You won't finish that stocking tonight."
"No . . . I shan't finish it."
[PAUSE]
"Yes, you were right. It's going to be wet tomorrow."

Like James's memory of his mother saying "We shall need a big dish tonight. Where is it—the blue dish?" which illustrates his belief that "she alone spoke the truth," the commonplace words are ironically remote from their emotional significance. But the novel does not insist on a simple opposition between the actual and the intangible. Very often, the spoken words sum up, rather than deflect the underlying meanings, as when the Swiss girl says "The mountains are so beautiful" or Mr Ramsay says "Damn you" to Mrs Ramsay or "Well done" to James. And colloquial phrases may take on a resonance beyond the control of the speaker. Mrs Ramsay, giving William Bankes a second helping of *boeuf en daube* at the moment of realizing that her dinner party has become a thing of "coherence" and "stability," says "Yes, there is plenty for everybody." The trite remark is suggestive of her bountifulness and creativity. Lily speaks of Mr Ramsay's landing at the lighthouse in an oddly uncolloquial sentence: "It is finished," she says, and then completes her picture. There is an irresistible suggestion of Christ's last words on the cross, not for any precise analogy but for the idea of sacrifice which they express. The first section of "Time Passes" eerily combines the sense of an ordinary conversation with prophetic notes: "It's almost too dark to see," says Andrew, involuntarily anticipating his own death.

Andrew's remark seems to hover between the spoken and the implied, as though it is hanging in the air. This effect contributes to the narrative method of the whole book, in which very many phrases and images seem only partly to be attached to the characters, so that their mental processes are fused with an impersonal voice, which takes over in "Time Passes." Such ambiguity in the creation of real characters applies, very often, to their spoken words, in that we are frequently unsure as to whether they are really spoken. Mr Bankes, one presumes, does not say "Nature has but little clay like that of which she moulded you" on the telephone to Mrs Ramsay. He says he will catch the 10:30 at Euston. Mrs Ramsay is far from saying "Nothing on earth can equal this happiness" to Mr Ramsay. Mr Ramsay does not actually step from the boat shouting "There is no God." Indeed, most of the characters are extremely inhibited. Mr Ramsay makes everyone very uncomfortable by *saying* "You find us much changed" or by bursting out with the lines from Cowper's "The Castaway." Lily's great cry for Mrs Ramsay, which reaches the level of the spoken word, is immediately an embarrassment to her: "Heaven be praised, no-one had heard her cry that ignominous cry." But the inhibition is not merely one of character; it reveals the immense difficulty of connecting the life of the mind and the world of external signs in any way that is at all meaningful: a difficulty that is central to Lily's attempt to paint. Because the appropriate utterances or signs are usually so much simpler than the complex of meanings they contain—"It is finished," or a line down the middle of the canvas—it is always necessary to understand that "Nothing was simply one thing."

The infusion of the commonplace with an enriching significance extends from words to things. Everyday matters of fact take on, largely through reiteration, the sort of resonance we have already seen apportioned to trite phrases. Thus the bill for the greenhouse roof becomes, in Mrs Ramsay's mind, a synecdoche for the whole corpus of material worries which have prevented Mr Ramsay, husband and father of eight children, from being also a first-class philosopher. The banging of doors, similarly, echoes throughout the book. Open doors and broken locks annoy Mrs Ramsay as she sits contemplating the shabbiness of the house; during the long, destructive onslaught of nature, the abandonment of the house by human agencies is accompanied by the ghostly banging of doors, and its undignified resurrection at the hands of Mrs McNab and Mrs Bast is, in part, a mending of doors:

> Attended with the creaking of hinges and the screeching of bolts, the slamming and banging of damp swollen woodwork, some rusty laborious birth seemed to be taking place . . . At last . . . keys were turned all over the house; the front door was banged; it was finished.

Though the house may have triumphed over death, its inhabitants, returning, have yet to work out their salvation. Without Mrs Ramsay, Lily feels it is "a house full of unrelated passions," suggested by "doors slamming and voices calling" and questions which "opened doors in one's mind that went banging and swinging to and fro." The image has come to stand for loss of control, and is used again by Lily in her memories of Mr and Mrs Ramsay's quarrels:

> He would whizz his plate through the window. Then all through the house there would be a sense of doors slamming and blinds fluttering as if a gusty wind were blowing and people scudded

about trying in a hasty way to fasten hatches and make things shipshape.

The major image here is of course that of the sea voyage, and the overlap between the real and the metaphorical is most obvious in the multiple significances which are drawn from the novel's island setting. In this *To the Lighthouse* resembles *The Voyage Out*; their titles could be run together, and suggest how close in both novels is the interrelationships between the external environment and the inner meanings. In *Mrs. Dalloway*, *The Waves* and *Between the Acts*, though there is great use of water imagery, the characters' lives are landlocked. But in *To the Lighthouse* "the sea is all about us": it dominates the actual and imaginative lives of the characters. An illustration of this is provided by the story Mrs Ramsay reads to James. In the fairy tale, the fisherman who has caught and released a magic flounder is urged by his bullying wife to ask the flounder for more and more exorbitant requests on her behalf: she must be king, emperor, pope, and at last God. Each request is granted to the accompaniment of a stormier sea, and at the final blasphemy the flounder sends them back to their original pigsty. The story can be read as a grotesque parody of Mrs Ramsay's protective, energizing relationship with her husband, suggesting that she is responsible for his constant need of reassurance: "perhaps it was her fault that it was necessary," and even that it is only her death which enables him to make his voyage: "There was no helping Mr Ramsay on the journey he was going." Or, its increasingly terrifying descriptions of the state of the sea might be used as analogies to Mrs Ramsay's periodic dread of the sound of the waves, which make her think "of the destruction of the island and its engulfment in the sea." Or the throwing back of the magic flounder might suggest the fish with a piece cut out of it, thrown into the sea on the voyage to the lighthouse like a sacrificial offering. Or the wife's blasphemy might carry a faint resemblance to Mr Ramsay's imagined words of triumph, "there is no God." These are fluid possibilities: the fairy tale is by no means meant to serve as a definite analogy to the novel. But they become possibilities by virtue of the consistent association between the sea and the lives of the characters.

Mrs Ramsay telling a fairy story to James, sitting at the window like a picture of a Madonna and Child (which Lily "without irreverence" may turn into a purple triangle), presides over a mythical world. Her powers seem to be those of a pagan goddess or a fairy-tale witch. But she has to work magic within the confines of the fierce, scientific world of real facts ruled by her husband, by Charles Tansley and by William Bankes: the masculine world of which Andrew would have been, and James will be, the inheritor.

To the Lighthouse continually hovers on the edge of becoming a fairy tale, or, more ambitiously, a mythical or even Christian allegory, whose subject—a frequent subject of myth—is the conquest of death.

Mrs Ramsay's mythical qualities seem to arise partly from her close involvement with the imaginative life of her children: the idea of the circus fills her with glee; as a child might, she hears in the waves a drum roll or a lullaby; the end of the fairy story is told as though in her own words; she fantasizes about the rooks, calling them Joseph and Mary, for her own pleasure as well as for the children; and her lullaby to Cam is a fairy story transforming reality into a mythical paradise which lingers in Cam's mind for life.

While her imaginings thus transform the real world into a story for children, she is seen by others as a superhuman figure with goddess-like creative powers. Dry, precise Mr Tansley finds himself singing a lyric paean to her beauty; Mr Bankes is moved to similarly exalted language: "The Graces assembling seemed to have joined hands in meadows of asphodel to compose that face." To Lily she is an "august shape" in whose heart "were stood, like the treasures in the tombs of kings, tablets bearing sacred inscriptions." In the mythic universe which Mrs Ramsay inhabits and Lily tries to recreate, all objects and characters may be transformed, as in a sea-change "in that underworld of waters . . . where in the green light a change came over one's entire mind." Prue, at the point of death, seems to Lily to become Proserpina, letting "her flowers fall from her basket." Augustus Carmichael, who druidically intones the mysterious poem at the end of the dinner, "holding his table napkin so that it looked like a long white robe," turns at the end into "an old pagan God, shaggy, with weeds in his hair and the trident (it was only a French novel) in his hands." Drugged and remote, evidently a man of vision, he becomes an acolyte at the ceremonies of creation engendered by Mrs Ramsay and Lily.

His trident concludes the association made throughout between mythic powers of creation and the powers of the sea, whose potential for enfranchising the solid universe from its apparently fixed boundaries is sinister as well as creative. Not surprisingly, the imagination tends towards monsters when thinking of the marine underworld, and its mythical inhabitants, the sirens, are emblems of danger for hardy seamen such as Mr Ramsay:

> Steer, hither steer your winged pines,
> All beaten Mariners!
> Here lie Love's undiscovered mines,
> A prey to passengers—

> Perfumes far sweeter than the best
> Which make the Phoenix' urn and nest.
> Fear not your ships
> Nor any to oppose you save our lips;
> But come on shore,
> Where no joy dies till Love hath gotten more.

So reads Mrs Ramsay, from an undistinguished seventeenth-century poem by William Browne of Tavistock, which identifies her with the insidious, beguiling elements of femininity. But Mr Ramsay, who is to be a triumphant, not a beaten mariner (and who is mainly associated with land imagery), resists the siren:

> The whole of life did not consist in going to bed with a woman, he thought, returning to Scott and Balzac, to the English novel and the French novel.

Few others can resist her power, particularly at the dinner party, where she appears as a pagan deity presiding over a sacrificial rite in which Paul and Minta are the victims, "led . . . Lily felt, to the altar." As Mrs Ramsay put "a spell on them all," the bowl of fruit becomes for her "a trophy fetched from the bottom of the sea," and the dish of *boeuf en daube* the celebration of "a festival," creating a sense of eternity. As the meal draws to a close the voices of people talking at the table "came to her very strangely, as if they were voices at a service in a cathedral . . . some Roman Catholic cathedral." Earlier betrayal by her love of rhythm and need for security into murmuring "we are in the hands of the Lord"—which she does not really believe—she now, more actively, creates her own service, her own church full of worshippers, which she knows will outlast her. Lily, recreating her in "The Lighthouse," felt as if a door had opened, and one went in and stood gazing silently about in a high cathedral-like place." The mythical and religious association allow a superhuman aspect to Mrs Ramsay's power of creating harmony and radiance, like a stroke of light laid over a chaotic waste of waters. Her ability to reconcile "scraps and fragments," culminating in the dinner scene, justifies the association with mythical deities: Mrs Ramsay is herself a creator.

The spiritualization of character hovers between the real and the abstract areas of the novel. Mr Carmichael's trident is also a French novel; but, at the other extreme, the mythical apparatus provides for an almost entirely impersonal presentation in "Time Passes." Through death and absence, character is merged with nature, and becomes the stuff of folklore and legend in the myth-creating minds of Mrs McNab and Mrs Bast. The section shows an advance on the attempt in *Mrs. Dalloway* to turn the characters into superhuman beings. The solitary traveller of Peter Walsh's dream, who is and is not Peter, encountering the figure of a woman who is and is not Clarissa, anticipates the "sleeper" of "Times Passes," the walker on the beach who tries to find some meaning in appearances, and whose search for hope is thwarted by the "brute confusion" of the universe. Peter's dream stands out oddly in *Mrs. Dalloway*. In *To the Lighthouse* the hovering vantage point of the "sleeper" is more firmly integrated into the impersonal fabric of "Time Passes." His quest for truth, set first against the pseudo-biblical rhetoric which describes the decay of the house ("Let the wind blow; let the poppy seed itself and the carnation mate with the cabbage") and then against the "wantoning memories" of Mrs McNab, ensures that though the Ramsays' house is almost entirely given over to "the fertility, the insensibility of nature" there is, nevertheless, a constant reminder of human consciousness. The walker on the beach is not Lily, but he anticipates and recalls Lily's attempts to find some "vision" affirmed in "the sea and sky."

The empty house in "Time Passes" is full of empty shapes.

> What people had shed and left—a pair of shoes, a shooting cap, some faded skirts and coats in wardrobes—those alone kept the human shape and in the emptiness indicated how once they were filled and animated . . .
>
> So loveliness reigned and stillness, and together made the shape of loveliness itself, a form from which life had parted.

Shapes imply space, an emptiness at the centre. The abstract relationship between shapes and space is vital to the novel. Lily's painting (unfinished in "The Window," begun again and finished in "The Lighthouse") creates, and then has to solve, this relationship.

> And so lightly and swiftly pausing, striking, she scored her canvas with brown running nervous lines which had no sooner settled there than they enclosed (she felt it looming out at her) a space. . . . What could be more formidable than that space?

Filling a space entails a sense of perspective. As the morning wears on, two parallel perspectives are achieved (the structure of the narrative making the double achievement seem simultaneously). As Mr Ramsay's boat nears the lighthouse and to those on board the land becomes "very small: shaped something like a leaf stood on end." Mr Ramsay drops his melodramatic pose of suffering and James and Cam are momentarily reconciled to him. The approach to the stark actuality of the lighthouse, like the approach to death, enables the complex land entanglements to be put in proportion. Meanwhile on shore Lily too discovers that "so much depends . . . upon distance." As the boat draws away she is more able to understand Mr Ramsay; as she tunnels through her picture into the past she finds that the time and space dividing her from Mrs Ramsay make it possible to find her again.

Lily's visionary translation of life into shapes is the culmination of a similar process carried on throughout the book, which constantly reiterates a tension between simple and complex shapes. The importance of the lighthouse in the first part, "The Window," lies not in itself, but in the stroke of light it throws in a circular sweep across space, seen through the frame of the window. To some extent this light is identified with Mrs Ramsay's creation of harmony and rhythm, and she herself appropriates it, as Clarissa does the bells of London, finding it expressive of certain qualities in herself and of certain moments in her experience (comparable to Clarissa's in their translation of sexual into emotional exaltation). Only in the third part is the lighthouse seen in its concrete shape, not as a beam of light but as a tower: Mr Ramsay's lighthouse. James makes the comparison:

> The Lighthouse was then a silvery, misty-looking tower with a yellow eye that opened suddenly and softly in the evening. Now—
>
> James looked at the Lighthouse. He could see the white-washed rocks; the tower, stark and straight; he could see that it was barred with black and white . . . So that was the Lighthouse, was it?
>
> No, the other was also the Lighthouse. For nothing was simply one thing.

Though different, the two personae of the lighthouse, tower and beam, are simple. All the simple shapes of the book—the dome shape which Lily associates with Mrs Ramsay and Nancy with Minta, the triangular shadow cast by Mrs Ramsay, the wedge shape of her dark and secret self, the line drawn down the middle of Lily's picture—give a sense of fulfilment and evoke the obscure, unapparent levels on which the personality works. In contrast with such simple shapes are found repeated references to twists, knots, nets, meshes and weaves: the shape of the active life of relationships in which people speak, judge, worry, laugh at each other, give parties and arrange things. Mrs Ramsay at the window is continually stretched between her deep-sunk contemplative life and the external demands made on her in the scene. The indivisibility of these two areas of experience is suggested by her knitting, which, like her life of personal entanglements, she resents ("making some little twist of the reddish-brown stocking she was knitting, impatiently") but can continue unconsciously while she sinks down into herself. Her inner simplicity is contrasted with the life of "strife, divisions, difference of opinion, prejudices twisted into the very fibre of being," which she deplores. But she herself "in active life" "would be netting and separating one thing from another." It is the active side of her which leads Lily to ask what it was "by which, had you found a glove in the corner of the sofa, you would have known it, from its twisted finger, hers indisputably?" Like a "phantom net" (Mrs Ramsay's image for the lights of the town) she "tangled" one's perceptions "in a golden mesh" and rejoices to think that "wound about in their hearts, however long they lived she would be woven."

The web of active relationships spun by Mrs Ramsay, and living on through "Time Passes" in the "ball of memories" unwound by Mrs McNab, is set against the less delicate knots in "The Lighthouse" that bind the family together under Mr Ramsay, like the knots tied and untied by Macalister's boy: "A rope seemed to bind him there, and his father had knotted it and he could only escape by taking a knife and plunging it." While James struggles in his bondage, Lily is trying to untie "a knot in her mind": to complete the picture and to understand the Ramsays. The knotty problem of balancing "this mass on the right and with that on the left" is also the problem of balancing the evidence about the Ramsays' marriage in order to arrive at a completed picture and a moment of vision. Essentially this can only be a moment—"The vision must be perpetually remade"—and at the moment of completion it is already past. "I have had my vision," Lily concludes, not "I have it."

What Lily arrives at is the proper balance of shapes; this is not an easy achievement and it is undertaken several times in the book. Mrs Ramsay's dinner party is shaped out of disparate entities—hostilities, reservations, her own reluctance to participate—into a coherent whole, whose ingredients are of the most trivial (talk about vegetable skins and coffee) but whose effect is nevertheless grand and transcendental, because it has come about by a creative effort. Like Lily looking at her picture when it is done, Mrs Ramsay looks back on her dinner party as something that takes on a new perspective as soon as it is completed:

> With her foot on the threshold she waited a moment longer in a scene which was vanishing even as she looked, and then, as she moved and took Minta's arm and left the room, it changed, it shaped itself differently; it had become, she knew, giving one last look at it over her shoulder, already the past.

The search for "significant form" must continue. A few moments later she is reading the Shakespeare sonnet in which the lover invests the beauties of April with the idea of his beloved:

> They were but sweet, but figures of delight
> Drawn after you, you pattern of all those.

The poem gives her a sense of completed form:

> There it was, suddenly entire shaped in her hands, beautiful and reasonable, clear and complete, the essence sucked out of life and held rounded here—the sonnet.

There are three analogous activities. In the poem, the lover gives added meaning to shapes by the force of his emotion, just as the poet has "shaped" the sonnet to be "beautiful and reasonable" through a creative effort. Mrs Ramsay, reading, makes sense of the shapes on the page. In miniature, the passage shows the sense of the whole novel. Acts which give form to life—even the cutting out of illustrations from the Army and Navy Stores catalog—are creative and humanizing. Without creative actions there is only space, like the space caused by death.

For Lily to say that "Love had a thousand shapes" seems vague and sentimental until it is put in the context of the idea that Lily and Mrs Ramsay are both "lovers" trying to create shapes of wholeness:

> There might be lovers whose gift it was to choose out the elements of things and place them together and so, giving them a wholeness not theirs in life, make of some scene, or meeting of people (all now gone and separate) one of those globed compacted things over which thought lingers, and love plays.

The greatest achievements are proportionate to the greatest intensity of emotion. This is felt particularly of Lily's concentration, which is analogous to Mrs Ramsay's and is used in order to recreate Mrs Ramsay:

> Mrs Ramsay saying "Life stand still here"; Mrs Ramsay making of the moment something permanent (as in another sphere Lily herself tried to make of the moment something permanent)—this was of the nature of a revelation.

Lily brings the mythical Mrs Ramsay back to life by her creative effort to fill space with meaning. Before she does it, all that she sees is "like curves and arabesques flourishing round a centre of complete emptiness." She feels that if the meaning of life can be asked for with sufficient intensity

> the space would fill; those empty flourishes would form into shape; if they shouted loud enough Mrs Ramsay would return. "Mrs Ramsay!" she said aloud. "Mrs Ramsay!" The tears ran down her face.

The passage derives its energy from the language of painting. Without that we might look askance at its emotional intensity. The last part of the novel is a delicate matter, which is made to work only by the very careful sustaining of an intimate relationship between Lily's yearning for Mrs Ramsay and her desire to get the painting right. The "return" of Mrs Ramsay—though well prepared for by the legendary, mythical qualities with which she has always been invested—is only acceptable if we can barely distinguish Lily's two impulses. To this end, when Mrs Ramsay does appear, she is there very much as a model for the picture. The moment of climax is moving because it is very quiet, and even ironic: Mrs Ramsay's "perfect goodness" to Lily included her complete disdain of the picture which now immortalizes her; this is Lily's triumph over Mrs Ramsay as well as her tribute to her.

> Mrs Ramsay—it was part of her perfect goodness to Lily—sat there quite simply, in the chair, flicked her needles to and fro, knitted her reddish-brown stockings, cast her shadow on the step. There she sat.

But the moment has three sides, not two. It also marks the arrival of Mr Ramsay at the lighthouse, where—as though encountering death—he momentarily assumes the heroic standards of behavior which have previously been used to satirize him, and at last inspires nothing but admiration:

> He rose and stood in the bow of the boat, very straight and tall, for all the world, James thought, as if he were saying, "There is no God," and Cam thought, as if he were leaping into space, and they both rose to follow him as he sprang, lightly like a young man, holding his parcel, on to the rock.

Mrs Ramsay appearing, Lily completing her picture and Mr Ramsay arriving at the lighthouse are all victorious over the impersonal powers of chaos and death through their concentration on the task in hand and through the intensity of emotion which they possess or inspire.

The book's conclusion, then, is a moral one. Like *Jacob's Room*, *Mrs. Dalloway* and *The Waves*, *To the Lighthouse* deals with the possibility of coming to terms with death. Lily's painting does not set up a romantic dichotomy between aesthetic consolation and mortal suffering. The artistic act involves suffering; it sums up the extreme difficulty of giving some moral coherence to the chaotic forms of reality;

> It was an exacting form of intercourse anyhow. Other worshipful objects were content with worship; men, women, God, all let one kneel prostrate; but this form, were it only the shape of

> a white lamp-shade looming on a wicker table, roused one to perpetual combat, challenged one to a fight in which one was bound to be worsted.

The artist here rejects the passive form of worship (such as Christianity) for what she considers a more arduous responsibility. So Leslie Stephen, saying, like Mr Ramsay, "There is no God," turned from the "muscular Christianity" of his early years to a rationalist philosophy of responsibility and endurance, but retained the Evangelical belief in "the supreme importance of the individual's relation to the good." In a novel which criticizes and mocks but finally finds admirable Mr Ramsay's bleak drama of endurance, the consolations offered for death are based on the real Mr Ramsay's principles. Completed forms, whether made from a social and family group, an abstract painting, or the journey to the lighthouse, create the only lasting victory over death and chaos. Such forms can only be brought into being by means of the arduous search for truth which is a necessary personal responsibility.

"The Deceptiveness of Beauty": Mother Love and Mother Hate in *To the Lighthouse*

Jane Lilienfeld

Virginia Woolf's previously unpublished memoir, *Moments of Being*, contains two essays which clarify not only the autobiographical origins of *To the Lighthouse*, but why Virginia Woolf was impelled to write that novel. In 1908 Virginia Woolf wrote the essay "Reminiscences" as an introduction to her family life. In this early essay, Virginia Stephen's mother, Julia, possesses all the perfections of a Shakespearean ingenue, with no flaws to make her real. To her daughter she appears as "a princess in a pageant," a vision, an impossible being. Such idealization seems to be a defense against great anger, and, indeed, this anger is admitted, examined, and tempered in the memoir, "A Sketch of the Past." Here the Stephen family unfurls in its magnificence and horror; a mother, ironic, quick, alarming, skeptical and ever-busy, not given to doting on her daughter Virginia, but tied to a husband whose demands she encouraged. Such a balanced picture of the fascinating and annoying Julia Stephen was possible only because Virginia Woolf had done "for myself what psycho-analysts do for their patients" in the writing of *To the Lighthouse*. The angers and grudges of years of family romance explode in *To the Lighthouse*, do their damage, and are reduced to artistically malleable proportions.

Virginia Woolf uses the characters of Mr. and Mrs. Ramsay in *To the Lighthouse* as surrogates for her own parents, Leslie and Julia Stephen. Buried deeply in the presentation of his personality, Mr. Ramsay's kindness and attachment to his family all but disappear as his tyrannical neediness looms over his being like the shadow of a massed cloud formation. Thus Leslie Stephen by implication is diminished to an emotional sponge. Nor is the light

From *Twentieth-Century Literature* 23, no. 3 (October 1977). © 1977 by Hofstra University Press.

turned on Julia Stephen as Mrs. Ramsay an altogether kind one. Delving deeply into her relations with her mother in "A Sketch of the Past," Virginia Woolf realized:

> The later view, the understanding that I now have of her position must have its say; and it shows me that a woman of forty with seven children, some of them needing grown-up attention, and four still in the nursery; and an eighth, Laura, an idiot, yet living with us; and a husband fifteen years her elder, difficult, exacting, dependent on her; I see now that a woman who had to keep all this in being and under control must have been a general presence rather than a particular person to a child of seven or eight. Can I remember ever being alone with her for more than a few minutes? Someone was always interrupting.

This analysis is true, balanced, exact. So judicious an analysis would not have been possible without the intervening creation of *To the Lighthouse*, a novel in which Virginia Woolf gave vent to the great anger and hurt that her relations with her mother had caused her. It is clear from "A Sketch of the Past" that the child Virginia Stephen felt the longing for and separation from Julia Stephen in exactly the way Lily Briscoe longs for and is cut off from Mrs. Ramsay. *Moments of Being* clarifies as never before that in the figure of the belittled Lily Briscoe, Virginia Woolf has put herself. To many critics, Lily Briscoe is an artist who must do in paint what the writer of the novel must do in the novel form; more than this, however, Lily Briscoe is herself a surrogate for the daughter, angry at her mother's commitment to others, a daughter who sustains her mother's death, and who lives beyond it to grow into her own personhood. This essay will examine in detail the relations between Mrs. Ramsay and Lily Briscoe as representative of those between a mother and a daughter.

More than a celebration of the wonderfulness of Mrs. Ramsay, *To the Lighthouse* is plotted to take the reader and characters through a successful reconsideration and rejection of Mrs. Ramsay's mode of life. At the beginning of the novel, Lily Briscoe timidly stands up to the imperious Mrs. Ramsay, saying "She liked to be alone." Lily Briscoe does not want to marry, but instead she wants to care for her father and to paint. Yet throughout the first part of the novel Lily Briscoe is so enmeshed in Mrs. Ramsay's powers that the painter cannot acknowledge consciously the depths of her anger at the older woman. By the end of her journey to the lighthouse, Lily has resolved many dilemmas for herself. She accepts her singleness, her need to paint. She accepts and acknowledges her hostility to Mrs. Ramsay's beliefs and machinations. Recognizing her love for Mrs. Ramsay, Lily moves beyond it to a love and respect for herself dependent on and integrated with her mature assessment of Mrs. Ramsay.

It is Virginia Woolf's genius to have re-created the process that a woman who wishes not to be the archetypal mother and wife must go through in order to separate herself from her almost overwhelming urge to fuse herself with such a mother. What happens to a woman who is not going to be an appendage or even a ruler of men, but who wishes to be a lonely looker within the self for sources of knowledge and satisfaction? Lily Briscoe's initiation into womanhood is the process by which she turns from the stranglehold of the archetype to an understanding that she may forge her own patterns of behavior which allow her spirit to achieve an independence and maturity unhoped for in her early fierce ambivalence.

Lily Briscoe's relations with Mrs. Ramsay appear tangential. Mrs. Ramsay can recognize Lily only by placing her in previously formed categories of women. Mrs. Ramsay summarizes Lily in one sentence and does not deviate from this view during the course of the novel: she thinks little of Lily's looks, less of her painting, knows she will never marry if left to her own devices, yet nevertheless likes that "flare of something" in Lily's independence. Comparing Lily to Minta Doyle, Mrs. Ramsay thinks that "at forty" Lily will be "the better of the two" (part 1, sec. 17; [all further references will be to part 1 unless otherwise indicated]). When she paints her final picture of the Ramsays, Lily is forty-four, Mrs. Woolf's age at the writing of the novel.

Lily Briscoe is no relation to Mrs. Ramsay. She has none of the privileges that Mrs. Ramsay's daughters have. She is not invited to live in the Ramsay's home for the summer, but must take rooms in town. Lily's knowledge of Mrs. Ramsay's ideas of her makes it difficult for Lily to assert herself against the older woman.

An outsider, Lily's position is all the more poignant given her great passion for Mrs. Ramsay. Like the other characters, Lily finds it impossible not to be drawn to this admirable woman of strength, resolution, beauty, gaiety. More specifically, Lily needs Mrs. Ramsay because she is a motherless spinster living in shabby respectability with an aging father. In her circumscribed life, Lily lacks the very thing she loves in Mrs. Ramsay, the principle of generativity, the need to turn like artichokes toward the sun, toward the heart of life.

Thus, as Helen Storm Corsa says, "It is in Lily that the largely libidinal attachment to the mother is seen. Her love . . . in its totality and in its idealizing force, dominates the first part of the novel . . . Her grief over the loss of the mother has long preceded the real loss of Mrs. Ramsay."

Autobiographically, then, Lily Briscoe is a surrogate daughter to Mrs. Ramsay through whom Virginia Woolf can explore with impunity some of her responses to her mother. The curiously belittled quality that Lily has (thinks Mrs. Ramsay in judgment, "Everything about her was so small" [sec. 17]), her reticence, her skimpiness seem at times to be almost a punishment on Lily and the author whom she represents for Lily's rebellious thoughts.

The author's decision to have someone other than the obedient and quiet Prue, the obvious Cam, the observant Rose, and the conscientious Nancy play a daughterly role to the Ramsays is an important one. Lily is an orphan, for her father is little more than an ornament with which to decorate several sentences about her. In Victorian fiction it is often the orphan to whom the quest is given, who has the heroic role, and who is the survival figure. Therefore it is appropriate that Lily have the last word, that the novel end with Lily's vision.

But the fact that Lily is essentially an orphan reveals something of Virginia Woolf's feelings about her place in her own family. Like Lily, she felt she had been deprived of mothering. She felt great psychological alienation from her mother, not having adopted Julia Stephen's role, Julia's career, Julia's attitude toward her own husband. She did not see herself as having Julia's charm, beauty, children, flocks of men adoring her (for all the men in *To the Lighthouse* except Mr. Carmichael are to some degree in love with Mrs. Ramsay). Thus, Lily Briscoe is a figure closer to the author's sense of herself than is Mrs. Ramsay.

Lily would be threatening to the mother if she were known to be as powerful a perceiver as she is. Certainly Mrs. Ramsay is not aware of Lily's secret powers, yet Lily is the only character who clothes Mrs. Ramsay in the appropriate shapes of imagery and whose penetration divines Mrs. Ramsay's thoughts. Painting her, Lily makes Mrs. Ramsay and James into a purple triangle, an equivalent to Mrs. Ramsay's own sense of herself "when invisible to others" as "a wedge-shaped core of darkness" (sec. 11). Lily rightly reads Mrs. Ramsay's expectations about her friendship with Mr. Bankes: "(oh, she's thinking we're going to get married)" (sec. 13). Mrs. Ramsay is thinking exactly that. Lily knows instantly at the dinner party when Mrs. Ramsay strays like a lost sailor, and when she returns, the sun striking her sails (sec. 17). Lily hears without words Mrs. Ramsay's plea that she smooth over Charles Tansley's social ineptitude. Indeed, "Lily Briscoe knew all that" (sec. 17).

These very powers mean that Lily must not be too near Mrs. Ramsay. She must not be her equal in daughterly rebellion against "always taking care of some man or other" (sec. 1). From a safe distance, Lily's looking up to Mrs. Ramsay and her refusal to marry do not upset the harmony of the Ramsay family life. If Lily were a daughter who felt as she does as violently as she does, there would be little chance of her winning either freedom to do as she pleased or the reader's sympathy for her endeavors. But as a timid outsider, Lily can be pitied for her loss of Mrs. Ramsay's admiration, her deprivation of the treatment Mrs. Ramsay would afford either her daughters or an adult whom she considered her equal.

Because the archetypal view of Mrs. Ramsay depends mainly on Lily Briscoe's emotional vision, I will analyze in some detail the mythic and psychological implications of the central passage in which Lily expresses her love for and relation to Mrs. Ramsay (sec. 9). "What was the spirit in her, the essential thing," wonders Lily, "by which, had you found a crumpled glove in the corner of a sofa, you would have known it, from its twisted finger, hers indisputably?" Lily fills out the figure who twists this glove, clearly seeing both Mrs. Ramsay's domineering wish to manage all lives around her, and her incomparable breathtaking ability to make all love her beyond the bounds of mortal flesh.

The shape that Mrs. Ramsay wears when Lily thinks of her at that point in the novel interweaves Mrs. Ramsay's characteristics as a maturely beautiful, intuitively gifted mother and housewife with qualities beyond those of a mere earthly being. Lily's longing for Mrs. Ramsay's meaning, more than human nature itself, is the only way she can partake of Mrs. Ramsay's essence until she can paint the picture which embodies her. What she desires is that which James and Mr. Ramsay want: to have this woman, in all her beauty and its meaning, hers and hers alone. The language of this passage, its rhythm, the intensity of its longing merge to create the anguish with which Lily feels her separation from the force which is Mrs. Ramsay's nature.

Lily's longings imply someone larger than life, a being whose essence is the motherly quality itself, an all-nourishing, life-giving archetype. Mrs. Ramsay takes on mythic qualities outside of Lily's thought, though Lily's perceptions are the primary mode of characterizing Mrs. Ramsay as archetypal. The level at which Mrs. Ramsay shrinks into "a wedge shaped core of darkness," the being she is at that moment in the narrative (sec. 11) makes her greater than her earthly self and more than the mother of a large family. There she is at one with the ocean whose waves lap to the rhythm of her thoughts. "Our apparitions, the things you know us by, are simply childish. Beneath it is all dark, it is all spreading, it is unfathomably deep." It is to this essence of the person without human shape or gesture, a being endless and enormous, of an elemental shape and creative force, that Lily turns her worship. Her longing to be sustained and buoyed up, enveloped by that source of life, is rightly represented so that the very language of the wish is the source of the insight which finds Mrs. Ramsay the archtypal force of life itself.

Knowing her exact relationship to Mrs. Ramsay, feeling her own littleness, Lily immediately becomes self-deprecating when she utters to herself any word of criticism about Mrs. Ramsay: "Mrs. Ramsay was wilful; she was commanding. (Of course, Lily reminded herself, I am thinking of her relations with women, and I am much younger, an insignificant person, living off the Brompton Road)" (sec. 9). Why is it acceptable to Lily that Mrs. Ramsay is high-handed with younger women? Why deprecate herself in relation to Mrs. Ramsay? Yet Lily cannot help feeling herself less a woman when facing Mrs. Ramsay's urgings that the painter has chosen the wrong road in life to follow: single, penniless, determined to paint.

> Oh, but Lily would say, there was her father; her home; even, had she dared to say it, her painting. But all this seemed so little, so virginal against the other . . . yet . . . gathering a desperate courage, she would urge her own exemption from the universal law; plead for it; she liked to be alone; she liked to be herself; she was not made for that; and so have to meet a serious stare from eyes of unparalleled depth, and confront Mrs. Ramsay's simple certainty that her dear Lily, her little Brisk, was a fool.
>
> (sec. 9)

This argument propels Lily into a long wonderment about Mrs. Ramsay.

In this passage, Lily has been remembering an incident in which Mrs. Ramsay and she sat up talking all night as the moon chalked the garden white. Mrs. Ramsay had imitated Charles Tansley, and Augustus Carmichael, and even William Bankes in a hilarious slapstick routine. Then she had become serious, reminding Lily that "she must, Minta must, they all must marry." Lily resists this vision with all the force of which she is capable. She is the only female figure in the novel to whom is given the courage to resist Mrs. Ramsay's urgings to marry. "Then she remembered, she had laid her head on Mrs. Ramsay's lap and laughed and laughed and laughed, laughed almost hysterically at the thought of Mrs. Ramsay presiding with immutable calm over destinies which she completely failed to understand. There she sat, simple, serious. She had recovered her sense of her now—this was the glove's twisted finger."

Lily's laughter is almost hysterical, such is the force with which Lily denies Mrs. Ramsay's power. But as if to prove that Lily has already been joined with Mrs. Ramsay in ways beyond her own imagining, the pronoun confusion shows clearly that the two women are momentarily indistinguishable. Who is simple and serious? Who "had recovered her sense of her now"? For a brief flash of reading time, the one to whom the pronouns refer could be either woman. Mrs. Ramsay's power to draw toward her the lives of others cannot be avoided.

As soon as Lily thinks she has grasped "the glove's twisted finger" in her hand, Mrs. Ramsay eludes her, "But into what sanctuary had one penetrated? Lily Briscoe had looked up at last, and there was Mrs. Ramsay, unwitting entirely what had caused her laughter, still presiding, but now with every trace of wilfulness abolished, and in its stead, something clear which the clouds at last uncover—the little space of sky that sleeps beside the moon."

Neumann tells us in *The Great Mother* that "to be taken on the lap is to be taken to the breast." It was there Lily had been resting even as she laughed wildly. Her laughter implies that she feels superior to the Mrs. Ramsay who "presided over destinies." Feeling superior, Lily has not admitted her desire to be nourished by Mrs. Ramsay; but, pressed to the woman's lap, Lily there wishes "to be caught, sucked in, enveloped, and devoured, seeking, as it were, the protecting, nourishing, charmed circle of the mother, the condition of the infant released from every care, in which the outside world bends over [her] and forces happiness upon [her]." These words are Jung's speaking of the passion for fusion with the mother's essence, which is the central meaning of Lily's longing. Picking her head up Lily loses that unity implied by the unclear pronoun reference; she severs her connection to the mother. Pulling back from Mrs. Ramsay, Lily sees that, far from demythologizing her through laughing at Mrs. Ramsay's desire for power, her own vision clothes the woman in more than human shape.

Mrs. Ramsay's straightforward self who calls Lily such pet names as "her little Brisk" has vanished. Instead, Mrs. Ramsay's "wilfulness," the clouds of her personality, are blown aside to discover "something clear as the space which the clouds at last uncover—the little space of sky that sleeps beside the moon." That form can be seen, according to Neumann, as "the original form of the Enthroned Goddess, and also of the throne itself." Mrs. Ramsay is the space, "one of the most important projections of the Feminine as a totality," but is also that which the space contains. In this case Mrs. Ramsay is seen as "the moon which is experienced as forming a totality with the background against which it stands out," one of the forms the mother often wears. Lily has not penetrated very far into the space of "the sanctuary," but she senses that what is inside is a mystery. The moon, like the distant mother, remains unexplained, only shown, as do the sources of Mrs. Ramsay's beauty and her strange powers, which are clearly visible, but beyond human grasp.

Lily questions the meaning of the moon and its sheltering space, the contents of the sanctuary, even as she tries to make clear to herself what she desires from this astonishing woman: "Was it wisdom? Was it knowledge? Was it, once more, the deceptiveness of beauty, so that all one's perceptions, half way to truth, were tangled in a golden mesh? Or did she lock up within her some secret which certainly Lily Briscoe believed people must have for the world to go on at all? Everyone could not be as helter-skelter, hand to mouth as she was. But if they knew, could they tell one what they knew?" (sec. 9). What does "it" refer to? The moon-shaped mystery, Mrs. Ramsay's face framed by the whitening sky as the dawn rises? Or is "it" the result of Mrs. Ramsay's beauty? Beauty's deceptiveness betrays Lily Briscoe. The journey to the truth of "it" is made impossible by an entangling net, a golden mesh which imprisons and restrains the journeyer. The ambivalent character of this image is essential. Mrs. Ramsay's beauty, protective as it may be, is such that it keeps one from wanting to go beyond it. Even so, in its Terrible aspect, does the beauty of the Great Mother take the form of nets and veils to ensnare those whom she refuses to let go. Mrs. Ramsay is herself almost conscious of this great force in her. Butting her chin on James's head as she reads him the fairy tale, she thinks "Oh, but she never wanted James to grow a day older! Or Cam either" (sec. 10).

Stopped at Mrs. Ramsay's flesh, Lily feels the meaning of it forever kept from her. The knowledge that they are both human beings with a sense of scattered selves Lily cannot admit, though this knowledge of similarity is the one form of unity with Mrs. Ramsay she has so far seen available to her. Lily thinks that Mrs. Ramsay cannot be as she herself is. She traps herself into looking to the mother for that for which she is herself responsible. Her longing not to let go, but to hold onto the essence of Mrs. Ramsay, forces her to enter the sanctuary, to seek that little space of sky which sleeps beside the moon.

> Sitting on the floor with her arms round Mrs. Ramsay's knees, close as she could get, smiling to think that Mrs. Ramsay would never know the reason of that pressure, she imagined how in the chambers of the mind and heart of the woman who was, physically touching her, were stood, like treasures in the tombs of Kings, tablets bearing sacred inscriptions, which if one could spell them out, would teach one everything, but they would never be offered openly, never made public.
>
> (sec. 9)

Desperate now, Lily returns again to a useless unity. "Close as she could get" is very far from her desires. Lily's imagination places the universe framing Mrs. Ramsay into Mrs. Ramsay's heart or womb. "The little space of sky which sleeps beside the moon" has become vacant rooms inside the beloved's heart or womb, a holy sepulchre. The moon has been elongated to great tombstone-shaped tablets. The extreme danger to the self that such longings as Lily has is apparent in the nature of the imagery. Lily cannot remain a suckling child dependent on the Mother for nourishment. Yet she longs for the food of life, created, stored, dispensed through the insides of the mother. These are the treasures of death, and the sacred vessel is a tomb. Mrs. Ramsay's manna is a stone with graven words. Nevertheless, though it might mean merging her own self, lost, into the other's being, Lily longs to penetrate that inner fortress even as she later desires to hurl herself headlong from a cliff while seeking Minta's missing brooch.

> What are was there, known to love or cunning, by which one pressed through into those secret chambers? What device for becoming, like waters poured into one jar, inextricably the same, one with the object one adored? Could the body achieve, or the mind, subtly mingling in the intricate passages of the brain? Or the heart? Could loving, as people called it, make her and Mrs. Ramsay one? for it was not knowledge but unity that she desired, not inscriptions on tablets, nothing that could be written in any language known to men, but intimacy itself, which is knowledge, she had thought, leaning her head on Mrs. Ramsay's knee.
>
> (sec. 9)

Retaining their ambivalent character of giving birth while promising death, the stone tablets of wisdom, those "treasures in the tombs of kings," have been rounded to great stone jars. As such they repeat the image of the shaping space which first surrounded the moon and then flowed inside to be the shape of Mrs. Ramsay's heart or womb. Round, made of earth, these jars hold the waters of life, the blood of the body, the milk of the breasts. But "treasures in the tombs of kings," these jars are also vessels of death, burial urns for the bones of the dead. Thus, through the imagery we see that Lily finds as tantalizing as death the inner space of Mrs. Ramsay's being. She wants to die out of one shape into another. She wants to be the life in Mrs. Ramsay's center. She wants to be the one to penetrate its holy place. She wants her body to be the one to mingle with that of Mrs. Ramsay. Inhabiting this woman's central core, Lily would become Mrs. Ramsay, replacing and killing her. Mrs. Ramsay's knees would serve as the doorways to the cave of birth and death for each woman. Inherent in this love is an aggression equal to it in insistence and intensity.

But offer as she might to Mrs. Ramsay her very self, that which she would never offer to another, Lily cannot renounce the bounds of her own being: "Nothing happened! Nothing! Nothing! as she leant her head against Mrs. Ramsay's knee. And yet she knew wisdom and knowledge were stored up in Mrs. Ramsay's heart. How then, she asked herself, did one know one thing or another about people, sealed up as they were?" Carnal knowledge, and the knowledge that comes from deep and open talk between equals, neither of these forms of union with the Mother can Lily attain. With one last cry of longing, Lily has withdrawn: "only like a bee, drawn by some sweetness or sharpness in the air, intangible to touch or taste, one haunted the dome-shaped hive, ranged the wastes of the air over the hives with their murmurs and their stirrings; the hives, which were people."

Neumann reminds us that "Bees are above all associated with Demeter, Artemis, and Persephone . . . [the bee] symbolizes the earth, its motherliness, its never-resting, artfully formative busy-ness." As a slave of the hive, Lily serves "the pure mother bee. And the bee priestess . . . must like the vestals and many other priestesses of The Great Mother, be virgins." Lily, small and insignificant, "living off the Brompton Road," virginal as her name and her desires protray her, is well symbolized by the bee, aspiring to give its honey to the Queen Mother, even as Lily longs to "reverence" Mrs. Ramsay's motherhood by her painting. "Mrs. Ramsay rose. Lily rose. Mrs. Ramsay went. For days there hung about her, as after a dream some subtle change is felt in the person one has dreamt of, more vividly then anything she said, the sound of murmuring, and, as she sat in the wicker arm chair in the drawing room window, she wore, to Lily's eyes, an august shape; the shape of a dome." Quickly the swift short sentences mimic Mrs. Ramsay's decisive movements. Lily has not achieved the longed-for union with Mrs. Ramsay. Exhausted, bereft, separate, Lily has removed herself. Yet her last sight of Mrs. Ramsay superimposes on the woman and the series of shapes she had worn in Lily's meditation. The ordinary back of the wicker arm chair still contains in it the form of the cave, vessel, tablets of stone, and moon rising from the horizon, all the forms the Great Mother wears.

The language functions superbly to re-create the emotions sweeping through Lily as she sees in Mrs. Ramsay form after form. The passage would lose its meaning if it were a reported dialogue between the women. For it must convey that which goes on beneath the consciousness of the characters. It must be seen as a projection of a mind overwhelmed by emotions which it but dimly recognizes.

The rhythms of the language which swirl around the figure into the climactic longings of "Was it wisdom? Was it knowledge?" and then subside into the disappointed murmurings of the final paragraph convey the proverbal implications of the passage as deeply as does the imagery. These words come from a part of Lily out of which she does not speak in ordinary discourse. Reticent, shy, reserved, the Lily who says "It grows cold," and "Will you take me with you?" does not seem possessed of the energy to form such grandiose streams of words. Here her language surges in her from a realm outside the rational. It is the language of the subconscious.

Readers of *To the Lighthouse* know that in this passage Lily Briscoe has been chosen to embody the central longings of all the characters for fusion with Mrs. Ramsay. Certainly the two other most demanding characters seek sustenance and inclusion in Mrs. Ramsay's mothering just as Lily does: James and Mr. Ramsay are ever turning to this woman for that which they will in the later part of the novel learn to find in themselves. For that is the movement of *To the Lighthouse*—how does one go beyond the mother who even while alive disappointed the desperate by keeping to and in herself the elusive sources of her being?

The anger at the Mother who denies her essence to her seekers is clear in the mythic imagery of the dinner party which clothes Mrs. Ramsay as the simultaneously Great and Terrible Mother. Once again, it is to Lily that this angry and mythic vision is entrusted. The dinner party is the scene wherein there is little difference between Mrs. Ramsay's appearance as The Great and Terrible Mother and her behavior as a successful Victorian hostess. The images which convey the mythic import of her actions arise naturally out of the situation.

Mrs. Ramsay begins her work of "merging, and flowing, and creating" by "sheltering and fostering the still feeble pulse as one might guard a weak flame with a newspaper" (sec. 17). She starts the fires of life which unite her guests in a fashion peculiar to herself: she pities Mr. Bankes and in rescuing him, she feels her creative energies flow toward him. The flame licking the newspaper suggests the central fires The Great Mother tends in her cave.

Similarly, Mrs. Ramsay's containing function as The Great Round, her relation to the sea, is clearly a part of her being. She is at once the sailor and "his ship": "Then she turned to William Bankes, smiling, it was as if the ship had turned and the sun had struck its sails again," thinks Lily as she feels Mrs. Ramsay once again become wholly present to her guests. Mrs. Ramsay is herself the container for the life she warms at her party, as the round vessel itself is a part of the manifestations of The Great Mother. The diners are the sailors, and the darkened sea on which they are perched makes their position precarious. Mrs. Ramsay encircles them, she protects them, but the small ship is no match for the turbulent sea which at any time may swamp the boat; and throughout the dinner party Mrs. Ramsay exerts her powers to the full to keep her guests unified and safe from "the watery vastness" outside the candle-lit windows.

Mrs. Ramsay has bid her children light the candles; their glow highlights her daughter Rose's gift to her, the beautifully arranged dish of fruit:

> What had she done with it, Mrs. Ramsay wondered, for Rose's arrangement of the grapes and pears, of the horny pink-lined shell, of the bananas, made her think of a trophy fetched from the bottom of the sea, of Neptune's banquet, of the bunch that hangs with vine leaves over the shoulder of Bacchus (in some picture), among the leopard skins and the torches lolloping red and gold. . . . Thus brought up suddenly into the light it seemed possessed of great size and depth, and was like a world in which one could take one's staff and climb hills, she thought, and go down into valleys.

This passage creates a space in which beauty and pleasure can occur. The "horny pink-lined shell" is like that manifestation of The Terrible Mother's awesome power, the vagina detenta, forbidding and destructive on the outside, tempting, soft, deliciously inviting inside. The fruits of the gods abound from it. This container is brought from the depths, wherein earlier Mrs. Ramsay had found her secret self, "something invisible to others" (sec. 11). The ordinarily hidden and mysterious is present, suddenly available to consciousness.

This world is given size and significance by the light which, like Mrs. Ramsay's earlier fire, is a source of life. The god of love, a hunter, reclines on the skins of conquered animals, fierce beasts with tearing fangs, the ranging appetities of love which the Mother has always at her command. Torches in the shell burn red and gold; like the shell itself, they could destroy, but tamed, they are beautiful, warming, joyous. Such is the Mother's power—that she may transform her most deadly aspects to protecting shelters for the spirit, so luxurious, indeed, that one rarely wants to leave their enclosures.

The "horny pink shell" becomes the dining room. Mrs. Ramsay has them all in her province, for "they were all conscious of making a party together in a hollow, on an island" (sec. 17). They are the group she has welded around the hearthfire, where her protecting round enables them to make "their common cause against the fluidity out there." So introduced, the central moment of the dinner party becomes simultaneously a ritual and an ordinary event. Minta Doyle and Paul Rayley had been late: "They must come now, Mrs. Ramsay thought, looking at the door, and at that instant,

Minta Doyle, Paul Rayley, and a maid carrying a great dish in her hands came in together." The dinner party will be a marriage feast: from the sacrifice entailed in the couple's union Mrs. Ramsay will nourish her guests.

Mrs. Ramsay hears Paul consecrate the event as he tells her of his union, saying with some difficulty the word "we": "'We.' . . . They'll say that all their lives she thought, and an exquisite scent of olives and oil and juice rose from the great brown dish as Marthe, with a little flourish, took the cover off." The two parts of the event merge into one sentence. The realistic sensual details create a satisfying dish, as well as an indication of the origin of the meal. "Olives, oil, juice" are an ancient festival food often sanctified by dedication to The Great Mother.

> The cook had spent three days over that dish. And she must take great care, Mrs. Ramsay thought, diving into the soft mass, to choose a specially tender piece for William Bankes. And she peered into the dish, with its shiny walls and its confusion of savory brown and yellow meats and its bay leaves and its wine and thought. This will celebrate the occasion—a curious sense rising in her, at once freakish and tender, of celebrating a festival, as if two emotions were called up in her, one profound—for what could be more serious that the love of man for woman, what more commanding, more impressive, bearing in its bosom the seeds of death; at the same time these lovers, these people entering into illusion glittering-eyed, must be danced round with mockery, decorated with garlands.

The realistic details of color, texture, smell which arise from the earthenware dish assure us that the dish is sitting on a believable table. Upper-middle-class Victorian woman that she is, Mrs. Ramsay has had servants to labor in the kitchen to produce this recipe of her "grandmother's." Her concern that Mr. Bankes get a special portion, too, reminds us that her vanity will be threatened if he is not overwhelmed by the meal. In all this behavior Mrs. Ramsay remains on the realistic plane.

Simultaneously her other self rises like a shadow towering over her seated figure at the table. "The great brown dish," with its "shiny walls" which shear off from profound depths, forms a vast cauldron, reminiscent of the great stone jars, the burial urns which Lily first perceived as tablets in Mrs. Ramsay's holy center. Its shape recalls the dish of fruit which was transformed through the imagery to house the party itself. Delicious in scent, the "soft" brown "mass" is somehow frightening and repelling, as if the meat in the dish were composed of the bodies of the couple who give themselves to love.

Mrs. Ramsay peers inside, almost, one has the sense, she looks into herself as the source of this manna. For it was in her round, in the family setting, in "the horny pink-lined shell" in the enclosure of ease, vacation, and happy bustling children and games that Minta and Paul found the space wherein to ramble and to fall in love.

Mrs. Ramsay here knows her powers. She knows that the lovers are lost to knowledge, glassy and "glittering eyed," revelers in a comic ritual, they are dazed by their ceremony. A woman well aware of the trials of marriage, Mrs. Ramsay is also The Great and Terrible Mother in whose space and under whose promptings Minta and Paul engage in this rite of transformation which causes death to the singular self.

> Now she was free both to triumph and to mock, she laughed, she gesticulated, till Lily thought, How childish, how absurd she was, sitting up there with all her beauty opened again in her, talking about the skins of vegetables. There was something frightening about her. She was irresistible. Always she got her own way in the end, Lily thought. Now she had brought this off—Paul and Minta, one might suppose, were engaged. Mr. Bankes was dining here. She put a spell on them all, by wishing, so simply, so directly. . . . Mrs. Ramsay exalted that . . . [this strange, this terrifying thing], worshipped that, held her hands over it to warm them, to protect it, and yet, having brought it all about, somehow laughed, led her victims, Lily felt, to the altar.

Lily understands that the powers of the Mother exact suffering, transformation, sacrifice. Lily's angry and frightened response to Mrs. Ramsay's exuberance in her own powers endows Mrs. Ramsay's actions with meaning beyond the personal. As always, Lily's response is crucial to her own characterization while at the same time giving, through the imagery which characterizes the intensity of her emotions, support to Mrs. Ramsay's mythic self. Left out, fading in the light of these raging fires, Lily resents that Mrs. Ramsay extends herself to Minta and Paul. At the same time Lily is the only one to recognize, as she did not in her earlier lament, that to give oneself over to The Mother is to give oneself beyond one's own life.

The way Mrs. Ramsay "forced her will on them" frightens Lily; "always she got her own way in the end" refers to the power of someone more than human. Lily knows that the source of Mrs. Ramsay's power is beyond her hostess' bidding, a power which surges through her radiant glance, her upright body, her vitality, and shows her in the service of that cause which uses her for its own ends. Fructifying, urging union, Mrs. Ramsay in her incarnation as The Great Mother has assured that "the species" will continue. Paul and Minta are to be melded into a new life; destroyed as individuals, pulverized into a "soft" brown "mass," Minta and Paul are the human sacrifice The Mother has exacted for the privilege of sharing her powers. The marriage "altar" is, by its very essence, as Lily senses, the place of human sacrifice.

So strong is Mrs. Ramsay's power that Lily offers herself up to it. Moved by Paul's beauty and his eagerness to seek Minta's missing brooch among the rocks where he proposed to her, Lily asks to go with him. Paul laughs in her face—imagine the effrontery of this unattractive woman to include herself on his dangerous quest! Humiliated and angry, upset at her offer and at the rejection of it, Lily turns to see whether Minta's role might be more to her liking. But the effects of Mrs. Ramsay's power are pervasive. Minta is flirting with Mr. Ramsay, who responds to her with warmth but who never even notices Lily Briscoe. The only way to deal with Mrs. Ramsay's power to kindle love is to denounce it. Lily resolves never again to submit herself to such pain; she resolves never to marry: "For at any rate, she said to herself, catching sight of the salt cellar on the pattern [to remind her of a change in her painting], she need not marry, thank Heaven: she need not undergo that degradation. She was saved from that dilution. She would move the tree rather more to the middle." This resolution enables her to finish out the meal in peace, but it is many years before the picture she had been planning reaches completion. Lily must, among other experiences, accept the rightness of her decision never to marry before she can finish her painting.

The threat implicit in the imagery of the union at the dinner party in part 1 is clear in Lily's memory in part 3. In the ten years after Mrs. Ramsay's death, Lily has witnessed the dissolution of Minta and Paul Rayley's marriage. It has become a partnership wherein each member lives a separate life. Minta accepts the fact that Paul has a mistress who shares his political concerns. She herself leads a full social life that does not include her husband. This marriage flouts Mrs. Ramsay's expectations for the Minta and Paul whom she united. Summoning up Mrs. Ramsay's spirit in memory, Lily triumphantly declares, "They're happy like that; I'm happy like this" (part 3, sec. 5). But the rupture of the Rayley's marriage was implicit in their union to begin with.

Early in the narrative Mrs. Ramsay admits to herself that she is by her very example urging Minta into marriage (sec. 10). She examines her heart: "a woman had once accused her of 'robbing her of her daughter's affections'; something Mrs. Doyle had said made her remember that charge again. Wishing to dominate, wishing to interfere, making people do what she wished—that was the charge against her and she thought it most unjust." It may be unjust to accuse Mrs. Ramsay of giving in to the promptings of her unconscious, but it is not wrong to say she led the couple into a false marriage. Just as her obvious wish for Minta influenced the young woman, so Mrs. Ramsay's expectations for Paul make their mark. Marrying Minta is for Paul an acceptable way to show his love for Mrs. Ramsay. Coming back from the harrowing task of becoming engaged, Paul thinks only of seeking out his hostess and telling her of his success. "I've done it Mrs. Ramsay; thanks to you" (sec. 14). In some obscure and perhaps unconscious way, Paul thinks he is marrying Mrs. Ramsay. What have Minta and Paul in common in part 1? Minta is a tomboy and Paul is a rather stupid and proper young man—they have only their love for their hostess as a bond. It becomes bondage under her expectant gaze.

Paul, Minta, and the Ramsay daughters, none escaped the power of the Mother to shape their lives. Even after her death, Mrs. Ramsay's modes of being are the only way her daughter Cam can handle her relations to her father and brother. For the ability to transcend the Mother is not something given; it is achieved only at great effort and suffering. Just as it was Lily earlier in the narrative who longed most volubly for the Mother, so it is her task in part 3 to find her own way, wrest herself free from Mrs. Ramsay's grip, and accept her own being on her own merits. That she is single, that she is a painter, that she has never married "not even Mr. Bankes" made Mrs. Ramsay dismiss Lily. These are the very facets of her character Lily learns to accept with joy.

Mysticism and Atheism in *To the Lighthouse*

Martin Corner

Virginia Woolf was an atheist: she was also a mystic. Both the mysticism and the atheism are there in some words that she wrote not long before her death. She is talking about the sudden shocks that life delivers, and of how she no longer finds in them "an enemy hidden behind the cotton wool of daily life"; instead, they are "a token of some real thing behind appearances. . . . From this I reach what I might call a philosophy . . . that behind the cotton wool is hidden a pattern; that we—I mean all human beings—are connected with this; that the whole world is a work of art. . . . But there is no Shakespeare, there is no Beethoven; certainly and emphatically there is no God" (*Moments of Being; hereafter referred to as MB*). The point of this article is to consider her atheism and her mysticism together; only in this way does it seem to me possible to understand either. I shall concentrate on *To the Lighthouse*, though this is not to imply that these issues are ignored elsewhere in her work. *The Waves*, in particular, touches on both. But the important connections and distinctions are at the center of *To the Lighthouse*; they enter vitally into Virginia Woolf's discriminations of character, as into her appraisal of the world that those characters inhabit.

II

The starting-point for discussions of mysticism in *To the Lighthouse* has usually been Mrs. Ramsay. This is understandable in that it is certain experiences of hers which are most immediately recognizable as mystical. But to concentrate on Mrs. Ramsay has the effect of emphasizing a kind of mysticism

From *Studies in the Novel* 13, no. 4 (Winter 1981).

which, I shall try to show, Virginia Woolf mistrusts and perhaps even rejects. Instead I shall start with Lily Briscoe; in her experience, and indirectly in Mr. Ramsay's as well, Virginia Woolf can be seen to trace a strain of mysticism of a quite different kind, one for which she has a much deeper sympathy.

When Lily sets about finishing her picture in the third part of *To the Lighthouse* she thinks about what she is doing through one image in particular: it is an image that expresses both what her art requires of her and what life as a whole demands. The image grows out of her feeling of risk as she confronts the "uncompromising white stare" of the blank canvas. As always when she turns from life to painting "she had a few moments of nakedness when she seemed like an unborn soul, a soul reft of body, hesitating on some windy pinnacle and exposed without protection to all the blasts of doubt." The figure on the pinnacle seems to be hesitating before a leap, and the leap is the making of the first mark on the canvas. That this is indeed what is intended is confirmed a little later, though here the reference is more inclusive and takes in life as a whole as well as painting: "Was there no safety? No learning by heart of the ways of the world? No guide, no shelter, but all was miracle, and leaping from the pinnacle of a tower into the air?" It is clear that the "leaping" image expresses for Lily the essence of her relationship with the world. The readiness to leap is the precondition of everything; without the leap of the brush there can be no picture, and without the leap away from safe understandings of the world, no life.

What is it that makes this desperate leap inevitable? Lily's understanding of painting offers an approach to the answer, though—like the leaping image itself—the point is generalized to take in all of life. For Lily, to face the blank canvas is also to confront "this formidable ancient enemy of hers—this other thing, this truth, this reality, which suddenly laid hands on her, emerged stark at the back of appearances and commanded her attention." "This other thing": Lily sees it most directly in the objects in front of her, in "this form, were it only the shape of a white lamp-shade looming on a wicker table" which "roused one to perpetual combat." Yet it is clearly more than form; it emerges "*at the back* of appearances" and it asks to be described in words such as "truth" and "reality." Nor is it something that passively allows itself to be observed: it suddenly lays hands on her and commands the disciplined attention of her art.

Lily has a similar experience a little later, but this time it has nothing directly to do with the painting of the picture. As she stands on the lawn she feels as though everything is approaching a point of comprehensibility. The world seems "dissolved . . . into a pool of thought, a deep basin of reality," and Lily feels that she is within reach of some conclusive revelation.

Perhaps if Mr. Carmichael were to join her in demanding an explanation of everything "something would emerge. A hand would be shoved up, a blade would be flashed." But Mr. Carmichael does not speak, and she dismisses all this as nonsense: the great revelation never comes. Then, involuntarily and inexplicably and with a sense of shock, she finds herself weeping: "Was she crying then for Mrs. Ramsay, without being aware of any unhappiness? She addressed old Mr. Carmichael again. What was it then? What did it mean? Could things thrust their hands up and grip one; could the blade cut; the fist grasp? Was there no safety?," and she goes on that all is "miracle" and "leaping from the pinnacle." What she hoped for has happened, but not in the way she wished. In her sudden painful awareness that there is no evading time and change, and that not even art provides a refuge, a hand is once again laid on her: the sword *is* thrust up, but not as a sign or explanation. Instead it cuts, and the fist grasps; whatever is "at the back of appearances" issues a summons that makes the leap inevitable.

This discussion has led into an area that can only be described as mystical. But it is important to be clear about the kind of mysticism that is involved here, and to see how it differs from the other kind which is familiarly associated with *To the Lighthouse* and in particular with Mrs. Ramsay. Varieties of mystical expereince have sometimes been categorized as "introvertive" and "extravertive": one turning inwards to the pure self, and the other outwards to the world, so that the mystic blends into a union with natural objects or with "Nature" as a whole. Broadly, the mystical experiences which Virginia Woolf describes in her fiction and her personal reminiscences are of the extravertive kind; as with Lily on the lawn, they occur as part of the interchange between an individual and the world around. The important distinction for Virginia Woolf is between two varieties of extravertive experience. On the one hand, there are moments that fit the definition just given, in which the self blends into unity with something else, a single object or the world as a whole. On the other there are experiences in which the self faces a reality which is of a different order from that given in commonplace awareness, something supremely worth attention, but yet remains quite distinct: no blending or merging takes place. One might call them, respectively, "fusing" and "facing" experiences.

Mrs. Ramsay's moments are predominantly of the "fusing" kind. When she is released from the pressure of activity an undifferentiated self emerges which absorbs or blends into certain objects (as, for example, the lighthouse); on other occasions she forges such a unity among those around her that she feels herself and them absorbed into a unity which is more than human, embraced and surrounded by a transcendental stability, "the still space that lies about the heart of things." Virginia Woolf accepts the reality and importance of such experiences, but she also sees danger in them. In the first place, they are momentary and involuntary: they fix points, but they do not mark out a path. As Lily comes to realize in part 3, "matches struck unexpectedly in the dark" do not cast their light very far. Secondly, and this is more decisive, these "fusing" experiences do not readily reveal their true nature; they are delusive, not in the sense of being unreal, but in that they tend to impose false interpretations. This can best be seen in Mrs. Ramsay when she sits down after the children have gone to bed. She looks toward the beam of the lighthouse, and feels that she is dissolved into it: "watching them in this mood always at this hour one could not help attaching oneself to one thing especially of the things one saw; and this thing, the long steady stroke, was her stroke. Often she found herself sitting and looking, sitting and looking with her work in her hands until she became the thing she looked at—that light for example." This blending of self and not-self gives Mrs. Ramsay an immense sense of security; there is no longer an opposing world set over against the self and threatening it. And it is out of this sense of security that the unexpected words well up into her mind: "We are in the hands of the Lord." But there is an immediate reaction: "instantly she was annoyed with herself for saying that. Who had said it? not she; she had been trapped into saying something she did not mean." She has been trapped partly by the traditional language for such experiences, but partly also by the experience itself. For these moments of "fusing," in which the gulf between man and the world disappears and the human blends with the nonhuman, have the effect of humanizing the world: nothing seems alien any more. And the step from this to the use of theistic language is an easy one, but one that Virginia Woolf refuses to take. Thus when in the passage quoted earlier she suggests that "the whole world is a work of art," she explicitly refuses to talk about an artist: "but there is no Shakespeare, there is no Beethoven; certainly and emphatically there is no God" (*MB*).

Mrs. Ramsay is equally emphatic: "How could any Lord have made this world?" It denies all the qualities that make us human: "there is no reason, order, justice: but suffering, death, the poor. There was no treachery too base for the world to commit; she knew that." The world constantly reminds us of its otherness, and it is this that makes theistic language impossible for Mrs. Ramsay. She is caught in a deep conflict here. On the one hand, her most vivid experiences are of a mystical unity with the world around her; on the other, she is forced into an atheist position by her awareness of an impassable gulf between the human and the nonhuman. But if this gulf is really quite impassable (and the rest of the novel, particularly part 2, seems to insist that it is), then how are these "fusing" experiences to be understood? There is no clear answer in *To the Lighthouse.* But a glance ahead to *The Waves* is helpful here. As he looks at the willow-tree, Bernard has an experience in certain respects similar to Mrs. Ramsay's as she looks at the lighthouse. He too attaches himself with peculiar intimacy to one object among many, and he finds in it the stability which Mrs. Ramsay also feels. The tree has a radiance which lifts it out of the everyday order of being and ensures that Bernard will remember it for the rest of his life: it is mystically perceived and it becomes a part of himself. But Bernard is able by the end of the novel to understand the intimacy of this experience more fully than Mrs. Ramsay understands hers. In retrospect he can give this account of his experience: "as I looked in autumn at the fiery and yellow branches, some sediment formed; I formed; a drop fell; I fell—that is, from some completed experience I had emerged." These moments are not, Bernard realizes, moments in which the self is diffused into other things; they are occasions of precipitation or condensation, in which the self uses other things to form itself. The object, tree or lighthouse, works as a symbol of this formation, and it is only through the discovery of the appropriate symbol that the formation occurs. They are moments when the self is "with sudden accretions of being built up, in a beech wood, sitting by a willow on a bank, leaning over a parapet at Hampton Court" (*The Waves*). She does not consciously make this analysis, but it is implicit in the way that Mrs. Ramsay comes to see the beam of the lighthouse after she has rejected "the hands of the Lord." It symbolizes herself, and in particular her honesty: "it seemed to her like her own eyes meeting her own eyes, searching as she alone could search into her mind and her heart, purifying out of existence that lie, any lie. She praised herself in praising the light." In these moments of "fusing" the self is merged with the object only insofar as the object becomes an enabling symbol of what the self now knows itself to be. The fusion is that of the symbol with its meaning.

In both *To the Lighthouse* and *The Waves* Virginia Woolf allows great importance to such experiences. But to have known moments in which objects become symbols and catalysts of our own meaning can feed a desire for the whole world "out there" to become symbolic and to repeat to us our own humanity; and to give way to this desire is, for Virginia Woolf, the mistake of theism. In *To the Lighthouse* this is made plain through the unnamed mystic of part 2. Summer brings him the promise of "cliff, sea, cloud, and sky brought purposely together to assemble outwardly the scattered parts of the vision within," and at such moments everything seems on the brink of becoming symbol. But the final clarifying fusion of world with human meaning never takes place; the mystic can never "read in the littered pieces the clear words of truth." What the anonymous mystic is trying to do is to extend momentary experiences of a "fusing" kind to the point of inclusive completeness, at which point the gulf between the human and nonhuman would disappear. But Nature fails to "supplement what man advanced," to "complete what he began." In the end the nonhumanity of the world is as terrifyingly apparent in its beauty as in its violence. "Violets came and daffodils. But the stillness and the brightness of the day were as strange as the chaos and tumult of night, with the trees standing there, and the flowers standing there, looking before them, looking up, yet beholding nothing, eyeless, and thus terrible." Such reminders of the world's irreducible strangeness and otherness constantly defeat the attempt to build an inclusive truth out of moments in which man and the world seem fused in a single meaning; and Virginia Woolf's atheism is, in essence, her determination to be faithful to that otherness. She is compelled, therefore, to distrust a variety of mysticism which tends always to cast over the world a reassuring tinge of human meaning.

III

Outside of the novels, though, most of Virginia Woolf's descriptions of mystical experiences are of the "facing," not the "fusing" kind; these, I shall argue, are intrinsically more compatible with her atheism, and bring us back to Lily on the lawn. Here is Virginia Stephen as a child in the garden of Talland House: "I was looking at the flower bed by the front door; 'That is the whole,' I said. I was looking at a plant with a spread of leaves; and it seemed suddenly plain that the flower itself was a part of the earth; that a ring enclosed what was the flower; and that was the real flower; part earth; part flower" (*MB*). Here there is no blending of subject with object, human with nonhuman; the child remains distinct, looking at the "real" flower which has suddenly become apparent to her. And though fuller and more consciously developed, Virginia Woolf's adult experiences take the same form. In February 1926 (while working on *To the Lighthouse*) she records that, as she walks through Russell Square, "I see the mountains in the sky: the great clouds; and the moon which is risen over Persia; I have a great and astonishing sense of something there, which is 'it.'" In September of the same year she talks about the object of her attention as an artist in a way that recalls Lily's frightening antagonist "at the back of appearances": "it is not oneself but something in the universe that one's left with. It is this that is frightening and exciting in the midst of my profound gloom, depression, boredom, whatever it is. One sees a fin passing far out" (*A Writers' Diary*; hereafter referred to as *WD*). In both instances the stress is on something "out there," apart from herself;

there is no hint of "fusing," nor is the language at all theistic. Even when, as in the following passage from September 1928, there is a suggestion of union with the "something," the union is prospective only, and not known in the moment of vision. She has come to Rodmell, and "got then to a consciousness of what I call 'reality': a thing I see before me: something abstract; but residing in the downs or sky; beside which nothing matters; in which I shall rest and continue to exist" (*WD*). In this, Virginia Woolf's clearest expression of the "facing" variety of mystical experience, there is a strong affinity with what Lily sees as she confronts her canvas. She too is aware of something not herself, "this other thing," which is "truth" and "reality"; which is there in the white lampshade, but yet is abstracted from it to emerge "at the back of appearances"; which more than anything else is worth her attention.

Yet there is one striking difference. Lily's "reality" challenges her to combat: hands are laid upon her, and the sword-blade cuts. She has no choice but to leap into a dangerous engagement. Virginia Woolf's "reality," on the other hand, stands quietly and unaggressively before her, promising not struggle and risk but rest and permanence. By the time that the picture is finished, however, the difference has become very much less. Lily's "vision" does in the end reach a point of rest and stability; how this comes about is best seen by looking at what happens in the completion of the painting.

As Lily begins to paint the sense of engagement with something commanding and uncompromising is very strong; her brush "was now heavier and went slower, as if it had fallen in with some rhythm which was dictated to her (she kept looking at the hedge, at the canvas) by what she saw." The image of the leap reappears, though this time instead of the tower Lily is walking the plank: "It was an odd road to be walking, this of painting. Out and out one went, further and further, until at last one seemed to be on a narrow plank, perfectly alone, over the sea." The sudden surge of feeling for Mrs. Ramsay seems to carry her off into the waves; but luckily no one has noticed, "no one had seen her step off her strip of board into the waters of annihilation." Once again, what is true of painting is true of life as a whole: it is all danger and risk.

As the picture develops, Lily's struggle is to keep two things in balance. She has a moment quite late on when she is convinced that her morning has been wasted: "she could not achieve that razor edge of balance between two opposite forces; Mr. Ramsay and the picture; which was necessary." Mr. Ramsay embodies something which is a condition of artistic success, but which her picture all too easily obscures and denies; and in this the picture is like Mrs. Ramsay. "What was the problem then? She must try to get hold of something that evaded her. It evaded her when she thought of Mrs. Ramsay; it evaded her now when she thought of her picture. Phrases came. Visions came. Beautiful pictures. Beautiful phrases. But what she wished to get hold of was that very jar on the nerves, the thing itself before it had been made anything. Get that and start afresh." Mrs. Ramsay and the picture have this in common, that they try to blend subject and object into a moment of vision, and by so doing they soften the otherness of the world. But Mr. Ramsay is an unwavering witness to the nonhumanity of the world; he therefore represents to Lily that otherness which must somehow be got into the picture if it is not to be false.

"Beautiful pictures. Beautiful phrases." The last words point ahead, once again, to Bernard in *The Waves*. Like him, Lily is made to see that there is something suspect in the power of any art—whether through paint or through words—to beautify the world and to translate it into human terms. She recognizes that her painting ought to preserve an awareness of the gulf between vision and the thing itself untransmuted; only by achieving this does art remain faithful to the distance between man and the world. Some artists, of course, neglect this; like Mr. Paunceforte they cultivate a reassuring idiom which they impose indiscriminately, so that the picture admits no distance between vision and object. But the true artist does not retreat into false humanization: Lily understands the need to work on the razor edge of balance between art and what precedes art, with all the risk that this involves. Any stroke of the brush may betray the vision or the world: every stroke is a leap into the gulf between the one and the other.

But it turns out that the leap is rewarded. The impossible happens: Lily discovers that by risking both vision and world she glimpses at least the possibility of securing both. Her picture is finished and she has her vision. But through the fidelity of attention which this demands of her she also sees the world with a directness and immediacy which calls from her the word "miracle." Just before the picture is finally resolved she feels that

> one must keep on looking without for a second relaxing the intensity of emotion, the determination not to be put off, not to be bamboozled. One must hold the scene—so—in a vice and let nothing come in and spoil it. One wanted, she thought, dipping her brush deliberately, to be on a level with ordinary experience, to feel simply that's a chair, that's a table, and yet at the same time, It's a miracle, it's an ecstasy. The problem might be solved after all.

The possibility of seeing the world as miracle and ecstasy is Lily's reward for the leap and the struggle. The miracle is not, however, a miracle of the extraordinary but of the ordinary. It springs from the attempt to see the world as it is in itself, unmolded to our humanity: "the thing itself before it has been made anything." It is toward this that Lily concentrates all her effort, and by the end of the morning she has come somewhere near achieving it.

Lily is striving for a perfect transparency of perception: "let nothing come in and spoil it." Insofar as she attains this she passes beyond the struggle and conflict to a moment of rest and stability which recalls Virginia Woolf at Rodmell. But in what sense can this be said still to be mystical? Earlier I related mystical perception to "a reality . . . of a different order from that given in commonplace awareness"; Lily, surely, is stressing the very reverse, the desire "to be on a level with ordinary experience." The whole discipline and concentration of the morning have been directed toward that transparency of perception in which commonplace things are what they are *and yet* are miracle and ecstasy, and so prove to be of a different order from that which ordinary experience imposed on them. This, and the supreme worth of the world so seen, establishes Lily's perception as genuinely mystical.

Lily's moment of vision is less a satisfactory ordering of the world than a discovery of the world as ordinary and yet transformed; it is this that makes art's ordering possible and truthful. What is revealed in that last moment of sudden clarity and intensity is supremely worth attention and the occasion of great joy, but the perceiver remains conscious of the distance between herself and what is perceived, does not blend or fuse with the world around her, and is not tempted to talk of it in theistic terms. Lily is, I would suggest, Virginia Woolf's fullest expression in this novel of the "facing" variety of mystical experience, a kind that is much closer to the heart of her view of the world than that with which we are familiar from discussions of Mrs. Ramsay.

IV

There are, then, two kinds of mystical experience in *To the Lighthouse*, one suggesting security and the other risk, one "the hands of the Lord" and the other the lonely figure on the pinnacle of a tower. There are also two kinds of atheism, and, as with mysticism, Virginia Woolf reveals a preference for one rather than the other. Mr. Ramsay's atheism is implied from the start; but, interestingly, it approaches explicit expression only at the very end of the novel, and then in connection with a "leap" which recalls Lily's as she stands before her canvas. The boat is about to reach the lighthouse: Mr.

Ramsay "rose and stood in the bow of the boat, very straight and tall, for all the world, James thought, as if he were saying, 'There is no God,' and Cam thought, as if he were leaping into space." In this moment the children see their father more clearly than ever before: to James, Mr. Ramsay's whole being proclaims its deepest truth. Why does Virginia Woolf wait so long before connecting Mr. Ramsay with an explicit declaration of atheism, and why does she make it so central a part of what he is at this culminating moment? It is, I would suggest, because she wishes us to see his atheism as something fully achieved only in this moment: something toward which his whole life has been a preparation.

The point is made clearer by a contrast, and one that is established very early in the novel. The only other explicit mention of atheism is to do with Charles Tansley, as he talks to James at the beginning of the book:

> "It's due west," said the atheist Tansley, holding his bony fingers spread so that the wind blew through them, for he was sharing Mr. Ramsay's evening walk up and down, up and down the terrace. That is to say, the wind blew from the worst possible direction for landing at the Lighthouse. Yes, he did say disagreeable things, Mrs. Ramsay admitted; it was odious of him to rub this in, and make James still more disappointed; but at the same time, she would not let them laugh at him. "The atheist," they called him, "the little atheist."

Tansley's atheism, suggested by the gesture of his skeletal hand, is made to seem petty, meager, almost sadistic; it is presented as a label, and consequently it seems superficial and assumed. And though Mrs. Ramsay is given a sympathy for Tansley which prevents her from condoning the children's mockery, there is in the passage a sense that Virginia Woolf is distancing herself from his intellectual position. For her, as for the children, he is "the atheist Tansley": his atheism is such that he can be stamped and categorized within three pages of the novel's opening, whereas it is not until two pages from its end that Mr. Ramsay's position is made explicit.

From this it is fair to conclude that Virginia Woolf's intention is to discriminate between atheisms just as she discriminates between mysticisms. There is the atheism of the "little atheist," a ready-made intellectual position which can be slipped into like an overcoat by a young man with his way to make in the world, which James and the other children instinctively mock; and there is the atheism which declares itself only at the end of a life and with such dignity that it transfigures the father in the eyes of his children.

Mr. Ramsay's life is an achievement of atheism; and the nature of this achievement brings his atheism into relation with the "facing" variety of mysticism that is there in Lily's completion of her picture.

Cam sees her father (*before* he springs from the boat) "as if he were leaping into space." The meaning of this is best understood by looking back over Mr. Ramsay's development as Virginia Woolf traces it in the third part of the novel. Mr. Ramsay's "leap" starts from a point quite different from Lily's. Hers begins as creative risk; it is what the "truth," the "reality" of art require of her. From that it broadens into a response to something "out there" which is aggressive and demanding, but which rewards those who do not attempt evasion with the miracle of ordinariness transfigured. Mr. Ramsay's leap, however, is essentially moral; it takes place not on a level of aesthetic attention but in his overcoming of certain moral limitations that are partly cause and partly consequence of an evasion of the world outside of himself. He is in no sense a mystic, and he never reaches the point at which a different order of being emerges. But though the word "mystical" is no longer appropriate, the idea of "facing" still is. Just as the "fusing" mystic may turn the world into a mirror of himself and so deny its otherness, in a parallel way atheism may be a form of egoistic lament, a preoccupation with a private despair which stands between the individual and the world. Mr. Ramsay has to learn to face the world and his position in it, and in particular to overcome the egoistic preoccupations that stand in the way of such a confrontation. His experience is a nonmystical analogue of the "facing" mysticism implicit in Lily's art.

"Has to learn to face the world": but surely Mr. Ramsay stands out from the start for his complete honesty in recognizing the otherness of the world and its nonhumanity? This is true; this is apparent on the second page of the novel, when he tells James that it will not be fine enough to go to the lighthouse. He cannot bear that people should deceive themselves about the world, and he suspects that his wife sometimes encourages self-deception. Intellectually, his atheist honesty and rigor are not in doubt. But morally the situation is different; here his atheism is at first not fully achieved. In his emotional life, and consequently in the way that he treats others, there are signs that he does not altogether accept what he admits intellectually. In his craving for reassurance and sympathy, and in his self-pity, there is a hidden outcry against the fact that he, directly and personally, should be a victim of the situation which he has, generally and theoretically, described. And in the assertiveness, at times almost the sadism, of his insistence of the inhumanity of the world, there is more than a trace of resentment that things should be as they are. It would not be altogether misleading to say that Mr. Ramsay begins as the kind of atheist who has not forgiven God for not existing; and such an atheism is incomplete.

He needs, then, to get beyond this stage and to accept the world as it is with everything that follows for his own position. Virginia Woolf hints at this early on when she makes Mr. Ramsay, for all his intellectual penetration, scarcely aware of the physical world around him. To Mrs. Ramsay it is as though he were "born blind, deaf, and dumb to the ordinary things, but to the extraordinary things, with an eye like an eagle's." He is not, in Lily's words, "on a level with ordinary experience"; he cannot say "that's a chair, that's a table" because his table is an abstraction, the object of the subject-and-object problems. He must learn to attend to the ordinary, and it is here that Scott helps him. What he enjoys in *The Antiquary* is above all "this man's strength and sanity, his feeling for straightforward simple things, these fishermen, the poor old crazed creature in Mucklebackit's cottage." But the learning cannot be done at second hand. Steenie's drowning is one thing: the death of Mrs. Ramsay, the drowning of the sailors in the bay, his own death and the obliteration of his works (anticipated in the drowning of Cowper's castaway), these are something else, and it requires a hard-won moral transformation to face an ordinary world which contains all this.

At the beginning of part 3 Mr. Ramsay's horizon is filled, understandably, with his grief at the death of his wife. As he stands with Lily on the lawn, he can see the bay and the lighthouse only as trivial distractions from the real matter in hand, his need of sympathy: "Why, thought Mr. Ramsay, should she look at the sea when I am here? She hoped it would be calm enough for them to land at the Lighthouse, she said. The Lighthouse! The Lighthouse! What's that got to do with it? he thought impatiently." For Lily, his very presence seems to drain ordinary things of their color and substance: "his gaze seemed to fall dolefully over the sunny grass and discolour it." But release comes, and it comes for both of them through an everyday object, Mr. Ramsay's boots. He notices untied laces, she the boots themselves, and she praises them, but with an immediate fear that she has committed the unforgivably triviality. She expects "complete annihilation," but "instead, Mr. Ramsay smiled. His pall, his draperies, his infirmities fell from here. Ah yes, he said, holding his foot up for her to look at, they were first-rate boots." To Lily, the boots are Mr. Ramsay; she is struck by how well they express the man. But to Mr. Ramsay they are simply boots, and in that entirely fascinating; and he delivers a brief lecture on boot-making, quite free for the moment from grief and self-pity. It is not just that he has been given something else to think about: in a small way he has discovered Scott's directness and ease with the ordinary world.

The effect of this is that, as he sets off with the children to the boat, Mr. Ramsay is transformed in Lily's eyes. To her "it seemed as if he had shed worries and ambitions, and the hope of sympathy and the desire for praise, had entered some other region, was drawn on, as if by curiosity, in dumb colloquy, whether with himself or another, at the head of that little procession out of one's range." He seems now to be looking outwards; to Lily it is at least a possibility that he is engaged with some reality apart from himself, "drawn on" in a way that parallels Lily's "exacting intercourse" with the reality "at the back of appearances." If Lily's intuition is right (and in part 3 the intuitions of other characters about Mr. Ramsay seem generally to be authoritative), a "dumb colloquy" has begun with something beyond his grief that is real and worth attention; Mr. Ramsay is beginning to move, though quite nonmystically, into a position which parallels that of the "facing" variety of mysticism.

But Mr. Ramsay still has a long way to go. Once in the boat he falls back into self-pity; he sees himself in imagination walking on the terrace of the house, alone: "he seemed to himself very old, and bowed. Sitting in the boat he bowed, he crouched himself, acting instantly his part—the part of a desolate man, widowed, bereft; and so called up before him in hosts people sympathizing with him; staged for himself as he sat in the boat, a little drama." He declaims, to Cam's significant embarrassment, "But I beneath a rougher sea. . . ." Gradually, though, he turns outwards again, and resumes the colloquy which Lily sensed on the lawn. Part of this is a continued approach toward the ordinary world, sometimes clumsy and scarcely disinterested (as when he asks about Cam's puppy) but sometimes natural and successful (as when he eats bread and cheese with the fishermen). It is most striking when he talks to Macalister about the great storm. James notices how "he leant forward, how he brought his voice into tune with Macalister's voice," and Cam hears "the little tinge of Scottish accent which came into his voice, making him seem like a peasant himself." His assimilation to the ordinary world is here almost physical.

But another aspect of this development, and one that Virginia Woolf links to this acceptance of the ordinary, is Mr. Ramsay's growing ability to face death without self-pity and the demand for others' sympathy. This is conveyed most forcefully at the moment when the boat crosses the spot where, in the great storm, three men were drowned. The children dread another self-pitying outburst, but instead "to their surprise all he said was 'Ah' as if he thought to himself, But why make a fuss about that? Naturally men are drowned in a storm, but it is a perfectly straightforward affair, and the depths of the sea (he sprinkled the crumbs from his sandwich paper over them) are only water after all." The sprinkling of the crumbs is particularly suggestive of acceptance; in its casualness it might seem cold and inappropriate, but yet it is a gesture which *by* its very casualness accepts the ordinariness of death.

In the last chapter of the crossing there are several details which emphasize in Mr. Ramsay a new openness and a new readiness to step outside the refuges of reassurance and sympathy. He lowers the book which has protected him from the turbulent emotions of the children; he sits there "bareheaded with the wind blowing his hair about, extraordinarily exposed to everything. He looked very old." To James, he seems like "some old stone lying on the sand," unprotected but strong enough now to need no shelter. He glances back toward the island which they have left, and we see him suspended between the "dwindled leaf-like shape" which is his past life and the unknown which lies ahead of him. He is drawing himself free of egoism and the accretions of personality, and in words that go beyond the physical situation Virgina Woolf tells us of his "complete readiness to land." There is in this an unflinching directness with the world and with death which is more than intellectual, which is reflected in the changed quality of his relations with the children, and which, in its own way, parallels Lily's desire to be "on a level with ordinary experience."

For Lily, the reward of success was to know the ordinary as miracle; for Mr. Ramsay too his new openness to "the thing itself" has its reward. We see him in these pages only through the eyes of James and Cam, but there are suggestions that their minds are increasingly in tune with their father's. Now that egoism and self-pity have abated, James's thoughts fall quite naturally into step with Mr. Ramsay's: for both of them "loneliness" is the truth of things. And at one point James almost echoes the "Castaway" outburst: "'We are driving before a gale—we must sink,' he began saying to himself, half aloud exactly as his father said it." The same intuitive understanding seems to be there in the last moments of the crossing: "they both wanted to say, Ask us anything and we will give it to you. But he did not ask them anything. He sat and looked at the island and he might be thinking, We perished, each alone, or he might be thinking, I have reached it. I have found it, but he said nothing." "We perished . . . ," offered without any of the earlier self-pity, is now a true recognition and not a complaint. "I have reached it" is corroborated by Lily in the last chapter, when she says "He must have reached it." Mr. Ramsay has had his reward. But what has he reached? It is not what he was struggled toward, the "Z" at the end of his philosophical argument. It is, however, presented as something equivalent, a matter of experience and not of philosophy; and it is clear that he could not have reached it if he had not been able to make himself "extraordinarily exposed to everything." Its nature is partly suggested by its coincidence with Lily's attainment of her vision: the two moments of fulfillment are sufficiently akin to be offered in parallel. Virginia Woolf is suggesting that here Mr. Ramsay reaches his vision (the vision of a mind very unlike her own, and so seen always from the outside), and the content of that moment is tentatively indicated in the last paragraph of section 13: "He rose and stood in the bow of the boat, very straight and tall, for all the world, James thought, as if he were saying, 'There is no God,' and Cam thought, as if he were leaping into space, and they both rose to follow him as he sprang, lightly like a young man, holding his parcel, on to the rock." In the eyes of his children Mr. Ramsay reaches a moment of transfiguration, from extreme age to youth, from dominance and coercion to a natural authority; and this has to do with the dignity and completeness, emotional as well as intellectual, of his atheism, which now for the first time finds clear expression. For Mr. Ramsay himself it is as though the truth of his life is now securely possessed: he discovers a new lightness and freedom in his release from egoism, and, once the leap has been taken and the "dwindled leaf-like shape" left behind, he finds an unexpected firmness in that nonhuman reality toward which the leap is directed. His feet land on the rock.

V

In the light of Mr. Ramsay's development, what is Virginia Woolf saying about atheism and its relationship to mysticism? As far as atheism is concerned, her central insight is that if it is to progress beyond the stage of the "little atheist" it must be a faithfulness, moral as well as theoretical, to the nonhumanity of the world. She presents it as a training of the whole person toward a comprehended truth, a truth which must be grasped emotionally as well as intellectually. And this is a process which involves risk; only when a person is able to leap from the pinnacle of the tower, away from whatever limited certainties are available—the self-protective ego, the familiar life—does the process achieve its fulfillment. And here a paradox appears which connects Mr. Ramsay with Lily, the atheist with the mystic. Without God, the leap ought to end in disaster, in the chaos of that void which Virginia Woolf evokes so powerfully in part 2 of *To the Lighthouse*. But those of her characters who succeed in facing the world nakedly and without evasion are shown to discover, mystically or otherwise, that they are not leaping into a void. Something emerges to meet them—the rock beneath Mr. Ramsay's feet, the reality "at the back of appearances," the ordinary world transfigured into miracle and ecstasy, and for Virginia Woolf herself that abstraction which nevertheless resided in the downs near Rodmell and beside which nothing mattered. This is the key to her atheist mysticism. For her, atheism was the renunciation of inappropriate expectations toward the nonhuman world; but it was also a condition of that purified perception which would reveal the world as ordinary and yet miraculous, as nonhuman in its otherness and yet beyond everything worth our attention.

Irreconcilable Habits of Thought in *A Room of One's Own* and *To the Lighthouse*

John Burt

There are two varieties of Virginia Woolf studies. One variety, which includes the studies of Auerbach, Naremore, Leaska, and others, describes Woolf's technical experiments. The other, represented by Marder, Heilbrun, Showalter, and Bazin, describes her ideology. The two varieties do not, however, represent opposing schools of opinion, for the authors of each type, rejecting the distinction between form and content, generously tend to derive the other type's conclusions from their own premises. Woolf herself lends authority to this procedure, for she equates the modernist novel with the androgynous sensibility she advocates, and argues that the Edwardian realist novel's dogmatism and concern with purely external detail is symptomatic of the moral and artistic decrepitude of the patriarchy.

The equation of feminist content and modernist form is misleading, for it connects certain political ideas with formal principles within which those ideas cannot be argued with integrity. If the modernist novel, as Woolf insists, must not be tendentious, but must instead record the impressions that fall upon the mind like an "incessant shower of innumerable atoms," then advocacy, even of those values necessary for writing such a work, can have no place within its "semi-transparent envelope." Were Woolf to preach in *To the Lighthouse*, she would, apparently, flaw that novel no less than the narrator's outbursts, according to Woolf, flaw *Jane Eyre*. How is it, then, that *To the Lighthouse* can be, as it is, at the same time an example of a form that has renounced overt persuasion and a powerful presentation of certain

From *ELH* 49, no. 4 (Winter 1982).

moral and political ideas that its author expects the reader to adopt? Form and content, it seems, are not only to be distinguished, they are to be opposed.

Perhaps our mistake is to assume that form and content must be consonant with each other, when in fact their dissonance may reflect those contradictions that artists, like everybody else, must, and yet cannot ever, resolve. Phyllis Rose has lucidly argued that the androgyny Woolf advocates in *A Room of One's Own* is, essentially, Keatsian negative capability described in sexual terms. I will discuss the arguments of *A Room of One's Own* and the themes of *To the Lighthouse* as examples of negative capability in their own right, describing both the formal and the ideological contradictions within which Woolf lives and writes, and estimating what, as an artist, she gains by remaining within them.

I

A Room of One's Own is primarily about the effects of women's poverty upon their art, but it is also about growing uneasiness between the sexes. When Woolf describes an ideal future, in which imaginatively androgynous writers will restore the romance of the past in a more perfect form, the two concerns merge. They diverge, however, when she evaluates the past: describing the emergence of women writers, she sees the past as a sort of dark age from which society has been painfully emerging; describing the collapse of romance, she sees the past as a vanished Eden. Even the idea of imaginative androgyny serves to separate the two major concerns of the book when it is applied to past art, for we learn towards the end of the book that the androgyny of past male writers is a product of the very circumstances that produced the economic and artistic subjection of women.

The central argument of the book might be summarized in five theses:

1. Patriarchal society imposes economic and social restrictions upon women on account of its own need for psychological support.

2. These restrictions limit the experience upon which art depends, causing creative women to suffer and depriving the general culture of their contributions.

3. As the material condition of women has improved, women writers have emerged, and the integrity of their work, its freedom from the scars and kinks of personal limitations, has risen in proportion to their status.

4. The rise of women has deprived the patriarchy of its psychological support, causing uncomfortable relations between the sexes that reflect themselves in the limitations of contemporary art.

5. When the emancipation of women is complete, a more adequate sex-

uality and a more adequate imagination, marked by androgyny or sexual openness, must emerge.

This argument depends upon a progressive view of human history, and an optimistic view, or at least a not tragic view, of human nature. The unhappiness of past eras is the result of the errors of past generations, errors defined in such a way as to make them easy to correct. It is one of the curious features of Woolf's theory of the origin of the subjection of women that that subjection is not motivated by men's will-to-power over women but rather by men's doubts about themselves; it is the creation of weakness searching for succor, not of strength searching for a victim:

> Women have served all these centuries as looking-glasses possessing the magic and delicious power of reflecting the figure of man at twice its natural size. Without that power probably the earth would still be swamp and jungle. . . . For if she begins to tell the truth, the figure in the looking-glass shrinks; his fitness for life is diminished. How is he to go on giving judgment, civilizaing natives, making laws, writing books, dressing up and speechifying at banquets, unless he can see himself at breakfast at twice the size he really is?

If there is bitterness in this passage, it is certainly not the bitterness one can find in *Three Guineas*. Contemptible as Woolf may find the pomposity she describes, she is more mocking than vituperative, and the sensitive egotists she describes seem more foolish than dangerous. If men oppress women not through joy of doing so but through weakness and self-doubt, we have no reason to suspect that progress is impossible, for we have no reason to suspect the men she describes of the bad faith that would make it so. Woolf's tone is critical, but also confident that the progress that such criticism is an attempt to bring about is not out of reach.

The underargument of *A Room of One's Own* presupposes a much less happy view of human nature and of history. This view is nowhere stated explicitly in the book, but the longing for the prewar era that colors the underargument is certainly a reaction against an unstated apprehension about human nature. As the critical tone of the major argument reflects optimism about the human prospect, so the nostalgia and tenderness of the underargument are signs of the half-hidden fear to which they respond. The underargument might be summarized as follows:

1. Men and women, before the war, could joyfully idealize each other.
2. This capacity for mutual joy accounts for the integrity, the imaginative life, of the art of the past, and can be identified with imaginative androgyny.

3. The war has destroyed this capacity entirely, but left us with a longing for it.

On the face of it, this argument, except for its mention of the war, seems to be simply a corollary to the argument concerning poverty and women. But to say that sexual uneasiness is caused by the lurid light in which men and women saw each other's faces in 1914 is very different from saying that this uneasiness is caused by the partial emancipation of women. For the slaughter at the Somme reveals far more than merely that Douglas Haig and his staff were ridiculous men of the sort Woolf satirizes above; the war reveals facts about human nature that makes every hope about moral advancement and progress mere wishful thinking. These facts, and not the sexual uneasiness they cause, are the burden of the underargument.

If the mention of the war as a possible cause of sexual uneasiness is brief and seemingly offhand, the fact of the war's destruction shapes, implicitly, the most distinctive feature of the underargument, the positive tone of its description of the prewar era. Although the major argument's description of this era, as we have seen, is far from strident, nevertheless it is clear that the old order was riddled with folly, that the future would certainly bring improvement, and that the present, for all of its discomfort, is a necessary stage in the bringing about of that improvement. The underargument, in contrast, not only idealizes the past in general (the positive features of which it hints are lost forever) but also idealizes the very sexual transaction that was the source of the problems the major argument was intended to solve.

The scene Woolf describes by way of noting what the current age has lost—the scene that illustrates how male artists of the past came upon the openness to the feminine that gave their works imaginative life—is simply a slightly spruced-up version of the scene that summarized the origin of the subjection of women. Male writers turned to women for support, and

> What they got, it is obvious, was something that their own sex was unable to supply; and it would not be rash, perhaps, to define it further, without quoting the doubtless rhapsodical words of the poets, as some stimulus, some renewal of creative power which it is in the gift only of the opposite sex to bestow. He would open the door of the drawing-room or nursery, I thought, and find her among her children perhaps, or with a piece of embroidery on her knee—at any rate, the centre of some different order and system of life, and the contrast between this world and his own, which might be the law courts or the House of Commons, would at once refresh and invigorate; and there would follow, even in the simplest talk, such a natural difference of opinion that the

> dried ideas in him would be fertilised anew; and the sight of her creating a different medium from his own would so quicken his creative power that insensibly his sterile mind would begin to plot again, and he would find the phrase or the scene which was lacking when he put on his hat to visit her.

The only difference between this scene, where a weary man is revivified by contact with the life of a woman, and the earlier scene, where an insecure man bolstered his morale by forcing a woman to reflect him at twice his actual size, is the tone of the narrator. For the events are identical. Through this presentation of its central transaction the underargument subverts the larger argument of which it is ostensibly a subsidiary part, and leads the book into a thicket of self-refutation from which there appears to be no escape.

What could have caused this reevaluation of the terms of the argument? What necessity compels Woolf not only to look with nostalgia and affection upon a past from which she and her whole society were trying to emerge, but also to idealize the very transaction that lay at the heart of the mistakes of that past? The sexual openness of the prewar years is never discussed as something present, but always as something lost. It is introduced, in the course of her description of the luncheon party she attended at Oxbridge, as a missing undertone:

> Before the war at a luncheon party like this people would have said precisely the same things but they would have sounded different, because in those days they were accompanied by a sort of humming noise, not articulate, but musical, exciting, which changed the value of the words themselves.

Woolf goes on to embody this murmuring in the love lyrics of Tennyson and Rossetti, lyrics the likes of which we no longer hear. The humming noise and the romance it represents are victims of the war. But, of course, they are not the only victims. For certainly the progressive argument, depending as it does on a sunny view of human possibilities, must also have died in the war. If Woolf does not say as much herself, it can only be because she sophistically displaces the war's destructive power from the progressive argument onto the idea of romance. Since the idea of romance and the possibility of androgyny seem to be related forms of imaginative openness, however, it is difficult to see what she gains by substituting a particular victim of the war, romance or androgyny, for the general victim, hope, unless it is enough that such a substitution gives the longing through which hope is to be rebuilt a particular and identifiable form.

The old order, destroyed by the war, then, is sacrificed in place of hopes that the war calls into question; and the value Woolf assigns to that order is its value as a sacrifice, a value created in retrospect by the destruction to which it is consigned. One of the elementary methods of surviving a catastrophe is to posit something valuable of which it has deprived us, so that by fixing our minds with longing upon what we have lost, we may give direction to our attempts to rebuild our lives. Destruction draws the sting from criticism of the old order, and the softening of criticism yields an ideal, even in that order's very shortcomings, that may guide us out of destruction. Only the need to answer the war's unspoken but looming objection could have necessitated such a radical reevaluation of the terms of Woolf's argument, could have led her to praise a transaction which she ought, by rights, to have criticized.

The reaffirmation of the values of the past that is so crucial to the underargument is a device to meet the danger posed to the book by the view of human nature that the war justifies. It is at the same time an ideal view of the human possibility, raised to meet the grave doubts about it that the war has caused, and a surrogate victim, which can be sacrificed in place of hopes about the future. The good Victorian past is a retrospective creation of the shadow of the war, just as the bad Victorian past is the creation of the sunlight of contemporary hopes. By idealizing the transaction that was the fundamental instrument of the subjection of women, Woolf takes back her argument in a limited way—and appeases the force of the unspoken argument of the war, which might otherwise have repealed a progressive essay entirely.

How the creation of the idea of lost romance might help a progressive view of history persist despite the war—by first displacing the war's destructive power, and then providing a focus for whatever regenerative powers we have at our command—might be summarized by means of a diagram:

Progressive argument
(Positive view of human nature)

Unstated total repeal of argument
(War makes a positive view of human nature impossible to believe)

Surrogate victim partially displaces repeal
(War makes romance impossible)

Shift of emphasis redeems surrogate victim
(The romance of the past is an ideal to be recreated)

Reaffirmation of progressive argument
(Romance will be recreated in a progressive way)

The introduction of the underargument allows the book to recover from the damage inflicted on it by the consciousness of the war, but the book continues to manifest the tension between criticism and nostalgia through which it recovered. This recovery does not take place by logical means—the progressive argument is repealed by the war as much at the close of the book as it was at the beginning—but it is too much to ask a book to argue a war away. It is enough if it can marshal those hopes and longings by means of which wars can be survived.

If *A Room of One's Own* recovers at all, then, it recovers through a brave sophistry. The two arguments of *A Room of One's Own* are not reconcilable, and any attempt to reconcile them can be no more than an exercise in special pleading. *A Room of One's Own*, however, is not an argument but, as Woolf proclaims in its opening pages, a portrayal of how a mind attempts to come to terms with its world. We find in the underargument that the world is perhaps not a place with which anyone could come to terms. Yet Woolf does not abandon those progressive hopes that she had wished to see realized, for even if the world is what she fears it might be, she knows that to abandon even dubious hopes would be a form of death, and that to hold fast to them, even in the face of what she knows, is a form of courage. The central contradiction in *A Room of One's Own* is the result not of weakness but of honesty.

II

It is traditional for critics of *To the Lighthouse* to juxtapose lists of masculine and feminine characteristics (using the Ramsays as representatives of their sexes) and to postulate that Art is a mediator between them. But beneath the tension between men and women is a different tension that cannot be resolved or repressed but only lived. We see this tension most clearly when we try to reconcile the progressive judgments the novel forces us to make with the far different conclusions forced upon us with equal urgency by the dark events, the deaths of characters we have loved, that form the thematic and structural center of the novel.

Where *A Room of One's Own* presents successive arguments that run in opposite directions, *To the Lighthouse* presents characters whose natures demand to be seen simultaneously from opposite points of view. Mr. Ramsay, for instance, is a more or less tyrannical representative of the old order, and we see him time and time again demanding sympathy and support in ways that we recognize from *A Room of One's Own* as being the stuff of which the subjection of women is made. Critics traditionally have taken a rather dim view of him, and their view is the counterpart in this novel of the progressive argument of *A Room of One's Own*. But Mr. Ramsay is not to be summed up so easily, and it is not simply the complexity of a convincing character that accounts for this difficulty.

Woolf's original conception of *To the Lighthouse* apparently included a much harsher version of Mr. Ramsay. Her entry in *A Writer's Diary* for May 14, 1925, describes her original idea for the novel:

> This is going to be fairly short; to have father's character done complete in it; and mother's; and St. Ives; and childhood; and all the usual things I try to put in—life, death, etc. But the centre is father's character, sitting in a boat, reciting We perished, each alone, while he crushes a dying mackerel.

This Ramsay is more self-pitying, more violent, and less human than the one we actually meet in *To the Lighthouse*. His self-pity speaks for itself. His crushing of the mackerel, an apparently pointless act, deserves a closer look.

In 1925, after she finished *Mrs. Dalloway*, Woolf wrote a series of short stories that were collected and published in 1973 under the title *Mrs. Dalloway's Party*. In one of these stories, "The Introduction," we meet a character named Lily Everit, who seems to be a younger and more vulnerable Lily Briscoe. When the story opens, Lily is standing alone at Mrs. Dalloway's party, knowing that Mrs. Dalloway is about to "bear down on her" and introduce her to "the world." As she watches Mrs. Dalloway come towards her, she clasps to herself, "as a drowning man might hug a spar in the sea," an essay she has written on the character of Dean Swift. Lily is not eager to be pushed into this "world," or, more specifically, into the old sexual order, and she describes to herself the role Mrs. Dalloway wishes her to play, in a figure that recurs in the story:

> All made her feel that she had come out of her chrysalis and was being proclaimed what in the long comfortable darkness of childhood she had never been—this frail and beautiful creature, this limited and circumscribed creature who could not do what she liked, this butterfly with a thousand facets to its eyes, and delicate fine plumage; and difficulties and sensibilities and sadnesses innumerable: a woman.

Mrs. Dalloway introduces the reluctant Lily to an arrogant young man named Bob Brinsley, in whose presence Lily fades. Her instinct, as she hears his monologue about his accomplishments and his belittling remarks about what he presumes to be hers, is to wish to destroy her essay, which earlier had been a bulwark she had opposed to "masculine achievement." As he rambles on about himself, Brinsley carelessly rips the wings off a fly. Lily reacts with a horror that completes her self-abasement and surrender; Brinsley's violence to the fly's wings shrivels the metaphorical wings upon her own back, converting them into the "weight of all the world."

The connection between the sadistic destruction of a small creature and the subjugation of women by men that we find in "The Introduction" was apparently also supposed to be made in *To the Lighthouse*. Mr. Ramsay, who crushes a mackerel, was to be similar to Bob Brinsley, who tears the wings off a fly. But in the novel as it was finally written, this act is transferred to a comparatively minor character. Macalister's boy, who accompanies Mr. Ramsay, Cam, and James on their trip to the Lighthouse in the last part of the novel. The act is still, perhaps, the climax of the book, but its meaning is vastly altered from Woolf's original idea of it.

The mutilation of the mackerel is described in a laconic paragraph enclosed in brackets—a paragraph like those that crop up in the "Time Passes" section of the novel. Like the parenthetical paragraphs of "Time Passes," it emphasizes the darkness and incomprehensibility of life we have seen hinted in *A Room of One's Own*. The scene interrupts and confirms the meditations of Lily Briscoe, who afterwards describes her state of mind immediately before as that of one who "steps off her strip of board into the waters of annihilation." On shore, working on her painting, Lily has begun to despair of making sense of her world, and she longs for Mrs. Ramsay, who has been dead for nearly ten years, to come back and give her the strength to struggle with life. She turns to Augustus Carmichael, an artist like herself, and, also like herself, someone rather out of the mainstream of sexual life, someone with whom she has a great unspoken affinity. Posing questions to him in her mind "about life, about death," she initiates a silent conversation with him that continues until the end of the book:

> What does it mean? How do you explain it all? she wanted to say, turning to Mr. Carmichael again. For the whole world seemed to have dissolved in this early morning hour into a pool of thought, a deep basin of reality, and one could almost fancy that had Mr. Carmichael spoken, for instance, a little tear would have rent the surface pool. And then? Something would emerge. A hand would be shoved up, a blade would be flashed.

Mr. Carmichael's unspoken response to Lily's question would be that everything but art vanishes, and it is in art that meaning must be found. Lily, in turn, seems to answer that all she can find in her art is her pain. Yet despite this, Lily's vision does not fade, but intensifies and darkens in character, revealing the central fact upon which art is based, what it takes to make beauty roll itself up and make empty flourishes form into shape. The shift to the boat where Macalister's boy mutilates the mackerel is not a shift away from the impending vision but the realization of that vision—in a way it is his knife that is the knife of the vision, and the reader learns (if Lily herself does not, since she doesn't see this scene) that the blade of the vision does indeed cut:

> Was she crying then for Mrs. Ramsay, without being aware of any unhappiness? She addressed old Mr. Carmichael again. What was it then? What did it mean? Could things thrust their hands up and grip one; could the blade cut; the fist grasp? Was there no safety? no learning by heart of the ways of the world? no guide, no shelter, but all was miracle, and leaping from the pinnacle of a tower into the air? Could it be, even for elderly people, that this was life?—startling, unexpected, unknown? For one moment she felt that if they both got up, here, now on the lawn, and demanded an explanation, why was it so short, why was it so inexplicable, said it with violence, as two fully equipped human beings from whom nothing should be hid might speak, then beauty would roll itself up; the space would fill; those empty flourishes would form into shape; if they shouted loud enough Mrs. Ramsay would return. "Mrs. Ramsay!" she said aloud, "Mrs. Ramsay!" The tears ran down her face.
>
> VI
>
> [Macalister's boy took one of the fish and cut a square out of its side to bait his hook with. The mutilated body (it was alive still) was thrown back into the sea.]

Only at this moment does Woolf abandon the narrative distance, the irony implicit in her multiple point of view narration, to join what she says in her own voice (within the brackets) to what she said (in indirect discourse) through Lily Briscoe. Woolf's parenthesis is the expression, even the fulfillment, of Lily's vision, as if the author took her cues from the character she has created rather than standing at a distance, evaluating and undercutting (as was her usual practice). Confronting the problem of the treachery and emptiness of life, Woolf and Lily are united in what my colleague Jonathan Freedman calls a "shared *cri de coeur.*"

The mutilation of the mackerel, which was originally intended to epitomize Mr. Ramsay and provoke the reader's hostility to him, instead becomes the symbolic center—shared by character, author, and reader—of grief over the death of Mrs. Ramsay. The concerns of the novel shifts from criticism to mourning, and as it does so our view of the characters we have been predisposed to scorn, like our view of the prewar era in *A Room of One's Own*, changes in a way nothing in the original idea, no matter how subtle or three-dimensional, could have led us to expect. This radical alteration of the novel's intent runs parallel to the alteration of *A Room of One's Own* two years later, and can be attributed to the same cause, to the necessity of confronting that collection of unhappy facts I have called the postwar argument.

III

Life's violence and life's meaninglessness are the central subjects of *To the Lighthouse*, and those passages where life is most unflinchingly seen—Lily's vision, "Time Passes," Mrs. Ramsay's reveries as a "wedge-shaped core of darkness"—are its greatest artistic tours de force. But it is not enough merely to confront the two chief terrors of life: they must be mastered, or at least survived. As in *A Room of One's Own*, it is in the old order, even in its shortcomings, that Woolf seeks the means of survival. Chastened and frightened by what the war proves about life, she idealizes the very transactions between men and women at which she had set out to scoff, and treats them not as the follies of an unenlightened age but as the attempts of that age to hold off the destructive forces by which it was finally overwhelmed. She returns to the Ramsays and their marriage, not abandoning her criticism, but adding a sympathy that springs as much from need as from nostalgia.

For all of its manifest problems, the Ramsays' marriage is carefully arranged to allow them to shield each other's different vulnerabilities; and strangely enough, it is by means of the very qualities that other characters criticize—the generosity that puts everyone in Mrs. Ramsay's debt, and Mr. Ramsay's bullying—that they are able to do so. Mr. Ramsay's fear is of aridity, and that fear takes two forms. First, he fears that he cannot live up to the demands of his heroic notions, that his most recent work of philosophy was not quite his best. This fear is compounded by the suspicion that the encumbrances of marriage and child-rearing have prevented him from doing the work he might have done had he remained single. Second, he fears that his efforts are not in the circle of life. Mrs. Ramsay—in a scene identical to that we saw both criticized and idealized in *A Room of One's Own*—seems able to respond to both fears, quieting his doubts and assuring him that he has not missed out on life.

Mrs. Ramsay, in contrast, fears the destructiveness and treachery of life, and she asks explicitly and apparently with authorial approval what was asked only implicitly in *A Room of One's Own*:

> How could any Lord have made this world? she asked. With her mind she had always seized the fact that there is no reason, order, justice; but suffering, death, the poor. There was no treachery too base for the world to commit; she knew that. No happiness lasted; she knew that.

Mrs. Ramsay's response to her uneasiness about life is to encourage people to take part in it; she seems to represent some of the very dangers she opposes: "There were the eternal problems: suffering; death, the poor. There was always a woman dying of cancer even here. And yet she had said to all these children, 'You shall go through it all.'" The concords that Mrs. Ramsay creates to meet life are of course themselves a part of life. Even the image Lily uses to describe the Ramsays' domestic happiness (which appears as she describes the freshness those around the Ramsays can feel after they have made up some differences between them) is disquietingly close to her image of life's terror, for the "blade in the air" she mentions is without doubt the blade that was thrust up in the course of her vision:

> All would be as usual, save only for some quiver, as of a blade in the air, which came and went between them as if the usual sight of the children sitting round their soup plates had freshened itself in their eyes after that hour among the pears and cabbages. Especially, Lily thought, Mrs. Ramsay would glance at Prue . . . assuring her that everything was well; promising her that one of these days that same happiness would be hers. She had enjoyed it for less than a year, however.

These sharp objects seem to cut two ways, representing at the same time how we enter life and how we counter life with means that are themselves a part of life.

Mrs. Ramsay's matchmaking protects her no more effectively than Mr. Ramsay's bluster protected him, and both activities are seen by the others as at the same time threatening and pathetic; but methods that do not allow them to protect themselves nevertheless do allow them, temporarily, to protect each other. Mrs. Ramsay's cultivation of life, as we have seen, subdues her husband's fear of lifelessness. Mr. Ramsay's uncompromising truthfulness subdues Mrs. Ramsay's fear of life's destruction as well.

Mr. Ramsay is well aware of what he calls his wife's sadness, and it seems to him that there is little that he can do about it:

> He could not help noting as he passed, the sternness at the heart of her beauty. It saddened him, and her remoteness pained him, and he felt, as he passed, that he could not protect her, and, when he reached the hedge, he was sad. He could do nothing to help her. He must stand by and watch her. Indeed, the infernal truth was, he made things worse for her. He was irritable—he was touchy. He had lost his temper over the Lighthouse. He looked into the hedge, into its intricacy, its darkness.

Mr. Ramsay shows a little more self-knowledge here than most readers (except Leaska) have given him credit for. It is a curious fact, however, that the harshness that he, along with most readers, condemns in himself is the very thing that protects his wife, for a moment, from life. The episode in which he expresses these doubts about himself is a case in point.

Mrs. Ramsay has just sent James to bed after telling him that they probably will not go to the Lighthouse the next day. When James departs she withdraws into herself and momentarily enjoys a delicious self-possession. She slips free of any particular time and place and becomes a "wedge-shaped core of darkness" that wanders throughout a world of shadowy suppositions, rather, as Auerbach has noted, like the author herself. Mrs. Ramsay becomes, as it were, a modernist narrator, an ally of the "little winds" of "Time Passes," and as she does so, she necessarily becomes subject to the nihilism that Auerbach notes as the universal concomitant of the modernist technique. The case of the narrator, for instance, exemplifies the danger of her method, for it is when she is most thoroughly free of the constraints of Realism—in "Time Passes"—that she most clearly identifies herself with that destructive and treacherous thing she refers to as "life," taking the point of view of an inhuman host of winds that replaces and destroys human observers:

> Almost one might have imagined them, as they entered the drawing room questioning and wondering, toying with the flap of hanging wall-paper, asking would it hang much longer, when would it fall? Then smoothly brushing the walls, they passed on musingly as if asking the red and yellow roses on the wallpaper

> whether they would fade, and questioning (gently, for there was time at their disposal) the torn letters in the waste-paper basket, the flowers, the book, all of which were now open to them and asking, Were they allies? Were they enemies? How long would they endure?

The destructive events in "Time Passes," that, like the mutilation of the mackerel, occur inside parentheses apparently obtruding into the text, in fact fulfill tendencies long latent in the figures of the passages they conclude. Just as the mutilation of the mackerel fulfill's Lily's vision, so the wartime deaths fulfill potentialities of the shadowy, siren-like lyric prose that they seem to interrupt:

> But slumber and sleep though it might there came later in the summer ominous sounds like the measured blows of hammers dulled on felt, which, with their repeated shocks still further loosened the shawl and cracked the tea-cups. Now and again some glass tinkled in the cupboard as if a giant voice had shrieked so loud in its agony that tumblers stood inside a cupboard vibrated too. Then again silence fell; and then, night after night, and sometimes in plain mid-day when the roses were bright and light turned on the wall its shape clearly there seemed to drop into this silence, this indifference, this integrity, the thud of something falling. [A shell exploded. Twenty or thirty young men were blown up in France, among them Andrew Ramsay, whose death, mercifully, was instantaneous.]

Like the narrator's, Mrs. Ramsay's meditations darken in character, and she apprehends life's treachery. But just at this moment, Mr. Ramsay passes by her and reproaches himself with his inability to protect her, and as he resolves not to interrupt her, she, knowing that he wishes to shelter her, stands up and goes to him herself.

When she goes to him, she is of course responding to his fear that he is outside of life, but her doing so enables him to respond to her own fear. It is contact with her husband's different nature that frees her from her melancholy, just as his contact with her freed him from his aridity:

> His arm was almost like a young man's arm, Mrs. Ramsay thought, thin and hard, and she thought with delight how strong he still was, though he was over sixty, and how untamed and optimistic, and how strange it was that being convinced, as he was, of all sorts of horror, seemed not to depress him, but to cheer him.

Even the domineering natural to one who "never tampers with facts" is later pressed into service against life:

> "You won't finish that stocking tonight," he said, pointing to her stocking. That was what she wanted—the asperity in his voice reproving her. If he says it's wrong to be pessimistic probably it is wrong, she thought; the marriage [Paul's and Minta's] will turn out all right.

The effect of Mr. Ramsay's asperity is to draw his wife from her unhappy musings, to recall her from a world Woolf always describes in the subjunctive to a world for which only the indicative is appropriate. This movement is, as Hartman has noted, a return from modernism to realism. The narrator often makes the same return, and for the same purpose: much as Mr. Ramsay protects his wife from life by insisting that she confine herself to what he sees as the facts, so Woolf herself repeatedly (and not always using Mr. Ramsay as an intermediary) protects her novel from the darkness that is its subject and motive power by returning to the narrative present of a traditional realist novel. This is not to say that Woolf returns from dangerous speculations to safer facts, for the facts are the violent events described in the bracketed passages that interrupt and confirm her most baleful speculations. Woolf returns not to the facts, but to the fictional conventions of Realism, just as Mrs. Ramsay returns not to the truth—for that is precisely what she is afraid of—but to the sustaining ignorance about life that she finds in her husband's inability to surmise. If the excursions out of the realist narrative present embody the source of the novel's power, then the return embodies what control Woolf is able to exercise over that power, and the discontinuity of the novel's form is a consequence of the complexity of its purpose. Just as *A Room of One's Own* partially redeemed the Victorian past in order to shield itself from the war, so *To the Lighthouse* partially redeems the realist novel in order to shield itself from the consequences of its central perceptions.

To the Lighthouse survives by returning to the very things—the realist novel and the old order—it had set out to discredit. But it is neither a realist novel nor a work of reactionary nostalgia, for in that case it would be a novel about delusions, not about mourning. Just as the progressive and postwar arguments stand side by side in *A Room of One's Own*, modifying each other and holding each other in check, so two irreconcilable assessments of the past stand side by side here. The survival of the novel's progressive ideology, an ideology critical of Mr. Ramsay, performs for the novel a function analogous to that Mr. Ramsay himself performs for his wife: it attempts to restrain, perhaps even to harness, the dangerous power provided by too clear a perception of life. The progressive ideology, however complicated by life's violence and meaninglessness, does for the content of *To the Lighthouse* exactly what the redemption of the realist conventions does to its form.

The attempt to restrain the dangerous but essential forces that drive the novel results not only in the explicit oppositions of Mr. and Mrs. Ramsay we have just seen, but also in the tensions between sympathetic and unsympathetic views of their marriage, between postwar and progressive habits of thought, and between realist and modernist forms of narration. The discontinuities within the content and the discontinuities within the form of *To the Lighthouse* are closely comparable and serve a common purpose: they allow the novel to pit a terrible life against the lifeless ability to master life.

To the Lighthouse is not an artifact, whose shape we can describe and whose meaning we can surmise, but a challenge to a continuous and difficult effort undertaken no less by the reader than by the author. It is not a thing, but an occasion; and to read it, we must partake of the author's effort to resist both those postwar habits that would devote it to death, and those progressive habits that would transform it from a work of art into a tract. We must resist, that is, the very destruction and aridity that the female and male characters, respectively, most fear. Woolf's concept of androgyny comes down to nothing more than this dual resistance. Whether her own resistance is successful we cannot say, for nothing succeeds until we can say "It is finished." Although Lily Briscoe may say this of her painting, Woolf can never say this of her novel. For it is in the nature of the effort it represents that it must not end.

Hume, Stephen, and Elegy in *To the Lighthouse*

Gillian Beer

> When my perceptions are remov'd for any time, as by sound sleep; so long am I insensible of *myself*, and may truly be said not to exist. And were all my perceptions remov'd by death, and cou'd I neither think, nor feel, nor see, nor love, nor hate after the dissolution of my body, I shou'd be entirely annihilated, nor do I conceive what is farther requisite to make me a perfect nonentity.
>
> (David Hume, *A Treatise on Human Nature*)

> Father's birthday. He would have been 96, yes, today; and could have been 96, like other people one has known; but mercifully was not. His life would have entirely ended mine. What would have happened? No writing, no books;—inconceivable. I used to think of him and mother daily; but writing The Lighthouse, laid them in my mind. And now he comes back sometimes, but differently.
>
> (The Diary of Virginia Woolf)

Several of Virginia Woolf's books compose themselves about an absence: Jacob's absence from his room, Mrs. Ramsay's in the second half of *To the Lighthouse*, and in *The Waves* Percival's in India and in death. Absence gives predominance to memory and to imagination. Absence may blur the distinction between those who are dead and those who are away. In one sense, everything is absent in fiction, since nothing can be physically there. Fiction blurs the distinction between recall and reading. It creates a form of immediate memory for the reader.

From *Essays in Criticism* 34, no. 1 (January 1984).

Writing about Hume, the philosopher he most admired, Leslie Stephen glosses his position thus:

> The whole history of philosophical thought is but a history of attempts to separate the object and the subject, and each new attempt implies that the previous line of separation was erroneously drawn or partly "fictitious."

In *To the Lighthouse* the fictitiousness of the separation between object and subject, the question of where to draw the line, is passionately explored, not only by the painter, Lily Briscoe, but by the entire narrative process. It is through Lily that the philosophical and artistic problem is most directly expressed and the connection between Mr. Ramsay and Hume first mooted. Near the beginning of the book, Lily asks Andrew what his father's books are about.

> "Subject and object and the nature of reality," Andrew had said. And when she said Heavens, she had no notion what that meant. "Think of a kitchen table then," he told her, "when you're not there."

In the book's last paragraph, remembering Mrs. Ramsay, looking at the empty steps, Lily at last solves the problem of the masses in her picture to her own satisfaction:

> She looked at the steps; they were empty; she looked at her canvas; it was blurred. With a sudden intensity, as if she saw it clear for a second, she drew a line there, in the centre.

The separation of the object and the subject, and the drawing of a line less erroneous, less "fictitious," than in previous attempts, defines the nature of elegy in this work. Virginia Woolf attempts to honour her obligations to family history and yet freely to dispose that history. In the course of doing so, she brings into question our reliance on symbols to confer value.

Virginia Woolf's other books imply aesthetic theories and draw upon the ideas of contemporary philosophers, particular Bertrand Russell's warning against assuming that language mirrors the structure of the world: "Against such errors" he writes in *The Analysis of Mind* (1921), "the only safeguard is to be able, once in a way, to discard words for a moment and contemplate facts more directly through images." That is an ideal and a difficulty which moves through Virginia Woolf's practice as a writer. Only in *To the Lighthouse*, however, is the power of philosophical thinking and its limitations openly a theme of the book. That has to do with the work's special nature as elegy.

In 1925, when she was beginning *To the Lighthouse*, Virginia Woolf wrote in her diary:

> I will invent a new name for my books to supplant "novel." A new —— by Virginia Woolf. But what? Elegy?

In elegy there is a repetition of mourning and an allaying of mourning. Elegy lets go of the past, formally transferring it into language, laying ghosts by confining them to a text and giving them its freedom. Surviving and relinquishing are both crucial to the composition of *To the Lighthouse*. Learning how to let go may be as deep a difficulty in writing and concluding a novel as it is in other experience.

The problem of achieving and of letting go is shared by mothers and artists. Mrs. Ramsay lets go through death. After her death the book continues to explore what lasts (how far indeed has she let go or will others let her go?). The novel questions the means by which we try to hold meaning and make it communicable.

> Meanwhile the mystic, the visionary, walked the beach, stirred a puddle, looked at a stone, and asked themselves "What am I?" "What is this?" and suddenly an answer was vouchsafed them (what it was they could not say).

All Virginia Woolf's novels brood on death, and death, indeed, is essential to their organization as well as their meaning. Death was her special knowledge: her mother, her sister Stella, her brother Thoby had all died prematurely. But death was also the special knowledge of her entire generation, through the obliterative experience of the first world war. The long succession of family and generation, so typically the material of the nineteenth-century roman-fleuve, such as Thackeray's *Pendennis* and *The Virginians*, or Zola's Rougon-Macquart series, becomes the site of disruption. The continuity of the family can with greatest intensity express the problems of invasion and even extinction.

Lawrence originally imagined *The Rainbow* and *Women in Love* as one long novel to be called *The Sisters*. But when the two books eventually appeared the first was a rich genealogical sedimentation, the second was thinned, lateral, preoccupied with a single generation. The parents in *Women in Love* are enfeebled and dying; the major relationships explored in the work are chosen, not inherited. In *To the Lighthouse* Virginia Woolf still tried to hold within a single work what Lawrence had eventually had to separate: the experience of family life and culture, before and after the first world war. She held them together by separating them. "Time Passes," like Lily's line, both joins and parts. It is one formal expression of the profound question: "What endures?" "Will you fade? Will you perish?," "The very stone one kicks with one's boot will outlast Shakespeare." "Distant views seem to outlast by a million years (Lily thought) the gazer and to be communing already with a sky which beholds an earth entirely at rest."

> "Ah, but how long do you think it'll last?" said somebody. It was as if she had antennae trembling out from her, which, intercepting certain sentences, forced them upon her attention. This was one of them. She scented danger for her husband. A question like that would lead, almost certainly, to something being said which reminded him of his own failure. How long would he be read—he would think at once.

This passage brings home the other anxiety about survival which haunts the book: how long will writing last? Mr. Ramsay's ambition to be remembered as a great philosopher registers some of Woolf's ambitions and longings as an artist too. They are expressed in another mode by Lily, who must complete her picture and complete it truly, but who foresees its fate:

> It would be hung in the attics, she thought; it would be destroyed. But what did that matter? she asked herself, taking up her brush again.

So the topics of the British empiricists, Locke, Hume, Berkeley,—the survival of the object without a perceiver, the nature of identity and non-entity, the scepticism about substance—lie beneath the activity of the narrative. They bear on the question of how we live in our bodies and how we live in the minds of others. Hume writes of mankind in general that

> they are nothing but a bundle or collection of different perceptions, which succeed each other with an inconceivable rapidity, and are in a perpetual flux and movement.

The emphasis on perception and on "flux and movement" is repeated in Virginia Woolf's writing. But, as I have already suggested, there was a more immediate reason for Hume's insistent and sometimes comic presence in *To the Lighthouse*.

When Hume is named in *To the Lighthouse* he is strongly identified with Mr. Ramsay's thoughts. He is first mentioned at the end of Mr. Ramsay's long meditation on the need for ordinary men and on their relation to great men (exemplified in the twin figures of Shakespeare and the "liftman in the Tube"). The section ends with Mr. Ramsay's self-defeated questioning of his own powers. Yet, he thinks:

> He was for the most part happy; he had his wife; he had his children; he had promised in six weeks' time to talk "some nonsense" to the young men of Cardiff about Locke, Hume, Berkeley, and the causes of the French Revolution.

His meditation had begun with the question: "If Shakespeare had never existed . . . would the world have differed much from what it is today?" The apposition of empiricism and revolution ("Locke, Hume, Berkeley, and the causes of the French Revolution") suggests a possible partial answer to that question, but it is self-deprecatingly framed as "some nonsense." The issue remains unresolved.

Hume's name next appears interrupting, and yet almost a part of, the current of thought generated by Mrs. Ramsay in section 11 as she thinks about "losing personality," eternity, the Lighthouse, and finds herself repeating phrases: "Children don't forget" . . . "It will end . . . It will come . . . We are in the hands of the Lord."

> The insincerity slipping in among the truths roused her, annoyed her. She returned to her knitting again. How could any Lord have made this world? she asked. . . . There was no treachery too base for the world to commit; she knew that. No happiness lasted; she knew that. She knitted with firm composure, slightly pursing her lips and, without being aware of it, so stiffened and composed the lines of her face in a habit of sternness that when her husband passed, though he was chuckling at the thought that Hume, the philosopher, grown enormously fat, had stuck in a bog, he could not help noting, as he passed, the sternness at the heart of her beauty.

Hume, philosopher of mind, has grown so absurdly substantial that he sinks into the bog. That physical episode becomes metamemory for Mr. Ramsay, who *sees* it, not having been there. The full story is reserved for section 13 when at the end:

> The spell was broken. Mr. Ramsay felt free now to laugh out loud at Hume, who had stuck in a bog and an old woman rescued him on condition he said the Lord's Prayer, and chuckling to himself he strolled off to his study.

Hume, the sceptical philosopher, is obliged to repeat the words of faith. We remember Mrs. Ramsay's involuntary "We are in the hands of the Lord." Communal faith usurps the individual will. At the end of this episode (sec. 13) Mr. Ramsay feels comfortable: Hume has been worsted. The giant towering above his own endeavours as a philosopher proves to be a gross man subsiding. For a moment he can be held to scale, contained in anecdote. But Mr. Ramsay is himself measured by his will to worst. The narrative engages with the difficulties that Hume's work raises. And by this means, as we shall see, Virginia Woolf movingly allows to her father, Leslie Stephen, within her own work, a power of survival, recomposition, rediscovery even.

Hume's presence in the work allows her to bring sharply into focus the question of what is "when you're not there," a topic traditional to elegy but here given greater acuity. In 1927 Bertrand Russell wrote in *The Analysis of Matter*:

> I believe that matter is less material, and mind less mental, than is commonly supposed, and that, when this is realized, the difficulties raised by Berkeley largely disappear. Some of the difficulties raised by Hume, it is true, have not yet been disposed of.

Hume's persistence, the fact that his difficulties cannot be disposed of, makes him a necessary part of the book's exploration of substance and absence, of writing as survival.

We know that Virginia Woolf read Hume, perhaps not for the first time, in September 1920. But his importance in *To the Lighthouse* is connected with his special value for Leslie Stephen. In the process of transformation from Leslie Stephen to Mr. Ramsay, Virginia Woolf notably raises the level of creativity and attainment at which the father-figure is working, placing him in the rearward and yet within reach of major philosophers. Whereas Leslie Stephen was a doughty thinker, high populariser, and man of letters, Mr. Ramsay is a possibly major, though self-debilitated, philosopher. This raising and enlarging sustains the scale of the father in relation to the writer and at the same time allows a process of identification between writer and father in their artistic obsessions. Virginia Woolf did not acknowledge having read much of Leslie Stephen's work. But when we turn to Stephen's *History of English Thought in the Eighteenth Century* (2 vols., 1876) the congruities between the themes of that work and *To the Lighthouse* are remarkable enough, and Stephen's actual exposition of Hume and the directions in which he seeks to move beyond him are closely related to the concerns of *To the Lighthouse*. The first of these is reputation and survival.

The first sentence of Stephen's book simultaneously places Hume at a pinnacle of achievement and presents the problem of literary reputation.

> Between the years of 1739 and 1752 David Hume published philosophical speculations destined, by the admission of friends and foes, to form a turning-point in the history of thought. His

> first book fell dead-born from the press; few of its successors had a much better fate.

The first section of the introduction is entitled "The influence of great thinkers" and it grapples with the question of how far the thinker thinks alone or as an expression of communal concerns. How does thought affect society? Stephen argues that

> the soul of the nation was stirred by impulses of which Hume was but one, though by far the ablest, interpreter; or, to speak in less mystical phrase, we must admit that thousands of inferior thinkers were dealing with the same problems which occupied Hume, and though with far less acuteness or logical consistency, arriving at similar conclusions.

Thinking is not exclusively the province of great thinkers, nor—more strikingly—are their conclusions different from others.

In *To the Lighthouse* Mr. Bankes suggests:

> We can't all be Titians and we can't all be Darwins, he said; at the same time he doubted whether you could have your Darwin and your Titian if it weren't for humble people like ourselves.

The relationship between "humble people like ourselves"—or not quite like ourselves—and great art, great ideas, great events, haunts and troubles *To the Lighthouse*. It is part of the work's deepest questioning of what will survive. The question includes the questioning of the concept of "great men," of indomitable achievement, of a world centered on human will, and extends to human memory and the material world.

> Does the progress of civilization depend upon great men? Is the lot of the average human being better now than in the time of the pharaohs? Is the lot of the average human being, however, he asked himself, the criterion by which we judge the measure of civilization? Possibly not. Possibly the greatest good requires the existence of a slave class. The liftman in the Tube is an eternal necessity. The thought was distasteful to him.

Stephen, pursuing the relationship between "great men" and the mass of thinking, writes:

> Society may thus be radically altered by the influence of opinions which have apparently little bearing upon social questions. It would not be extravagant to say that Mr. Darwin's observations upon

> the breeds of pigeons have had a reaction upon the structure of society.

Abstract thought and social action seem at times in *To the Lighthouse* to be polarised between Mr. and Mrs. Ramsay, but most of the thinking in the book is sustained by the activity of laying alongside and intermelding the separate thought processes within individuals in such a way that the reader perceives the connections which the characters themselves cannot. The interpenetration of consciousness in language on the page allows us to think through problems of substance and absence unreservedly.

In his analysis of Hume's thought Stephen gives particular emphasis to the idea of fictionality. Stephen writes:

> The belief that anything exists outside our mind when not actually perceived, is a "fiction" . . . Association is in the mental what gravitation is in the natural world.

(Lily's floating table is anchored by association, not gravitation, we remember.)

> We can only explain mental processes of any kind by resolving them into such cases of association. Thus reality is to be found only in the ever-varying stream of feelings, bound together by custom, regarded by a "fiction" or set of fictions as implying some permanent set of external or internal relations . . . Chance, instead of order, must, it would seem, be the ultimate objective fact, as custom, instead of reason, is the ultimate subjective fact.

There are obvious connections with *To the Lighthouse* in such an emphasis on reality as an "ever-varying stream of feelings." "Life," he writes in his discussion of Hume, "is not entirely occupied in satisfying our material wants, and co-operating or struggling with our fellows. We dream as well as act. We must provide some channel for the emotions generated by contemplation of the world and of ourselves."

Stephen, with Hume, affirms chance and custom rather than order and reason as the basis of perception. Nevertheless, such affinities with Virginia Woolf's writing appear at a very general level and need not imply any particularly intense recall of Stephen's work or conversation. If such consonances were all, I would feel justified only in calling attention to similarity, rather than implying a process of rereading, replacing. However, the actual examples that Stephen selects are so crucial in the topography of *To the Lighthouse* as to suggest that Virginia Woolf's writing is meditating on problems raised in the father's text.

In the novel there is an extraordinary sense of the substantiality of people. The children are always pelting here and there; words like "plummeting," "darting," "full tilt," express the *impact* of the body. We are, in the moment, in our bodies, and that makes the moment both the most substantial and the most ephemeral of all experiences. We are never for more than a moment in the same place, the same time, in our bodies. That gap between body and time fascinates her in *To the Lighthouse*. And so does the question of substantiality and its nature. Hume remarks:

> A substance is entirely different from a perception. We have, therefore no idea of substance.
>
> That table, which just now appears to me, is only a perception and all its qualities are qualities of a perception.

In *To the Lighthouse* we read:

> "Think of a kitchen table then," he told her, "when you're not there."
>
> So she always saw, when she thought of Mr Ramsay's work, a scrubbed kitchen table. It lodged now in the fork of a pear tree, for they had reached the orchard. And with a painful effort of concentration, she focused her mind, not upon the silver-bossed bark of the tree, or upon its fish-shaped leaves, but upon a phantom kitchen table, one of those scrubbed board tables, grained and knotted, whose virtue seems to have been laid bare by years of muscular integrity, which stuck there, its four legs in the air.

For the reader, pear-tree and table are poised equally as fictive images. The oddness of their conjunction makes us especially aware of them as images in the mind, though Lily's hefty imaginative work concentrates on the individuality of the table as perceived object (scrubbed, grained and knotted) even more than on the tree (silver-bossed bark, fish-shaped leaves). By her imaginative effort she lurches the table *beyond* table, into some moralised and comically anthropomorphic form. "Virtue" is shifted from being a question of essence, or of meaning, to one of moral endurance. Lily sees the table *upside down* so that it becomes humanoid, its legs in the air, bare and muscular, a table of integrity, naked but not violated.

This inversion of the generalised image expresses through comedy the artist's urge towards the particular and the substantial. And yet the major process of Lily's picture throughout the book is *away* from representationalism towards abstraction, as though only pattern finally can satisfy and survive. At the book's end the line in the centre of her picture is distanced almost as far as it is possible to go from the particularity of the tree with which she began. It is almost entirely free of reference. But it was generated out of the referential. The narrative does not itself show any sustained parallel movement away from the referential towards the purely lexical, but it does move away from the burdened authority of symbolic objects. That movement of creativity seems to bear on the function of Virginia Woolf's parents in the work of art she composes, and on the means by which we all seek to make things last.

Table, house, tree and stone: those four objects, and particularly the first two, are crucial to the narrative and the play of associations in *To the Lighthouse*. Discussing the problem of the relationship between idea and language Stephen remarks in his essay on Hume:

> Looking, in the first place, at the external world, nothing seems simpler than the idea corresponding to the name of an individual object, man, or tree, or stone.

But he adds:

> The man and the tree change visibly at every moment; if the stone does not change so rapidly, we discover that its qualities are at every instant dependent upon certain conditions which vary, however slowly. All things, as the old sceptics said, are in ceaseless flux; and yet, to find truth, we must find something permanent.

Man, tree, stone: much of the emotion and thought of *To the Lighthouse* moves through those objects, surrounded by the "ceaseless flux" of the sea. Mr. Ramsay meditates on enduring fame and its vicissitudes:

> The very stone one kicks with one's boot will outlast Shakespeare. His own little light would shine, not very brightly, for a year or two, and would then be merged in some bigger light, and that in a bigger light still. (He looked into the darkness, into the intricacy of the twigs.)

Hume sees the attempt to escape from the self into a wide world to free ourselves of our own perceptual constraints as inevitably doomed, and Stephen quotes a famous lyrical passage from Hume to illustrate this:

> "Let us fix our attention out of ourselves as much as possible. Let us chase our imagination to the heavens, or to the utmost

> limits of the universe; we never can really advance a step beyond ourselves, nor can conceive any kind of existence but those perceptions which have appeared in that narrow compass. This is the universe of the Imagination, nor have we any idea but what is there produced."

Stephen at this point abruptly turns the argument and opens a new paragraph thus:

> Yet it is a plain fact of consciousness that we think of a table or a house as somehow existing independently of our perception of it.

"A table . . . A house" begin to suggest more fully the way in which technical daring and emotional homage combine in *To the Lighthouse*, particularly in "Time Passes." The empty house, flooded with darkness, has been relinquished by its human inhabitants: "there was scarcely anything left of body or mind by which one could say 'This is he' or 'This is she'." No perceiver is there to see the house. The darkness or forgetfulness, death, absence, enters the house. "Certain airs" ask of the wall-paper "would it hang much longer, when would it fall? . . . How long would they endure?" At the end of the third section "Mrs. Ramsay having died rather suddenly the night before," the airs advance in anthropomorphic order, "advance guards of great armies," to meet "only hangings that flapped, wood that cracked, the bare legs of tables."

The material world is here sustained by writing, but it is a kind of writing which deliberately obliterates any suggestion of a single perceiver. Language draws attention to its own anthropomorphism, its habit of remaking objects in the image of human perception, the impossibility in Hume's words of "conceiving any kind of existence but those perceptions which have appeared in that narrow compass."

Near the book's conclusion, in the section which comes close to ghost story, Mrs. Ramsay appears to Lily as Lily strives to resolve her picture:

> One must keep on looking without for a second relaxing the intensity of emotion, the determination not to be put off, not to be bamboozled. One must hold the scene—so—in a vise and let nothing come in and spoil it. One wanted, she thought, dipping her brush deliberately, to be on a level with ordinary experience, to feel simply that's a chair, that's a table, and yet at the same time, It's a miracle, it's an ecstasy.

The precision and obduracy of artistic feeling rejects any raising, or symbolising, though it floods the ordinary with ecstasy. Lily's old experience of longing, "to want and want and not to have," itself at last becomes

> part of ordinary experience, was on a level with the chair, with the table. Mrs. Ramsay—it was part of her perfect goodness to Lily—sat there quite simply, in the chair, flicked her needles to and fro, knitted her reddish-brown stocking, cast her shadow on the step. There she sat.

Physical (she casts a shadow as no ghost can do), revenant, actual, unhaloed and unalloyed by symbol, she "simply" knits her reddish-brown stocking. Absence and substance momentarily resolve.

Earlier in the work Lily had intensely, though fleetingly, seen Mr. and Mrs. Ramsay as "symbolical," "the symbols of marriage, husband and wife." The moment of transcendence sinks down again and concludes with the anecdote I earlier quoted:

> Still for one moment, there was a sense of things having been blown apart, of space, of irresponsibility as the ball soared high, and they followed it and lost it and saw the one star and the draped branches . . . Then, darting backwards over the vast space (for it seemed as if solidity had vanished altogether), Prue ran full tilt into them and caught the ball brilliantly high up in her left hand, and her mother said "Haven't they come back yet?" whereupon the spell was broken. Mr. Ramsay felt free now to laugh out loud at Hume, who had stuck in a bog and an old woman rescued him on condition he said the Lord's Prayer, and chuckling to himself he strolled off to his study.

The repertoire of associations is richly at work here: the tree, so freely moved in the course of the book between substance, metaphor, thought, art, until at last it becomes line without reference. (Is Lily's final line tree or lighthouse? By then it no longer matters.) Here the tree figures as space, looking up they saw "the one star and the draped branches." In Hume's phrase, they "chase their imaginations to the heavens" until solidity has vanished, but immediately Prue runs "full tilt into them." There is an extraordinary joyousness in that substantiality, the warmth and prowess of the body is regained, and regained as comedy. Mr. Ramsay immediately turns to his enjoyment of Hume stuck in the bog and the moment can dissolve as they all take their separate ways. Living, here, means letting things be, holding them a moment, "a brilliant catch," then letting them go. The "symbolical" is valuable only if it is not freighted with permanence.

In this novel Virginia Woolf most acutely polarises the sexes. Never again in her later novels was the binarism of male/female, husband/wife, father/mother allowed predominance. Instead, in works like *The Waves* and *Between the Acts*, she creates a spectrum of gender, a fan of possibilities. In *To the Lighthouse*, however, the formalisation of difference is crucial to the activity of the novel. It is her homage to symbol, to generation, and to parenthood, but it represents also the "writing out" of the symbolic weight of parenthood. It is tempting, in considering difference, and the polarisation of sex-roles, to see Lily Briscoe as some sort of Hegelian third term, representing the artistic resolution of sexual fracture and contradiction. But geometric patterning offers a false stability of reading, a judging optimism, which serves to protect the reader against the evanescence studied in the work. That emphasis on evanescence requires a reappraisal of the authority of symbol.

To the Lighthouse is a postsymbolist novel. By this I mean that symbolism is both used and persistently brought into question. The act of symbolising is one of the major means by which in language we seek to make things hold, to make them survive. But above all, it is the means by which we make *things* serve the human. Symbol gives primacy to the human because it places the human at the centre, if not of concern, yet of signifying. Symbol depends for its nature on the signifying act. By its means concepts and objects are loaded with human reference.

Though *To the Lighthouse* is weighted with the fullness of human concerns, there is a constant unrest about the search after a permanence which places humanity at the centre. This search manifests itself in many ways: as continuity, through generation; as achieved art object; as storytelling; as memory; as symbol.

Language can never be anything but anthropocentric. In this book, Virginia Woolf struggles not only with the deaths of her father and her mother but with the death of that confidence in human centrality which was already being abraded in her father's generation by evolutionary theory. When Stephen attempts to move beyond Hume he does it by means of evolutionist arguments, emphasising the progressive, the developmental in the theory. The "race" is Stephen's new element (and it is an element that Virginia Woolf turns to, much later, in *Between the Acts*):

> Hume's analysis seems to recognise no difference between the mind of a man and a polyp, between the intellectual and the merely sensitive animal . . . the doctrine that belief in the external world is a "fiction" is apparently self-destructive. If all reason is fiction, fiction is reason. Modern thinkers of Hume's school meet the difficulty by distinguishing between the *a priori* element in the indi-

> vidual mind and in the mind of the race. Each man brings with him certain inherited faculties, if not inherited knowledge; but the faculties have been themselves built up out of the experience of the race.

Stephen moves away from individualism to a confidence in communal development. *To the Lighthouse* brings into question all such attempts to propose a stable accord between inner and outer, past and present, to seal the contradiction of subject and object through symbol.

> Did Nature supplement what man advanced? Did she complete what he began? With equal complacence she saw his misery, condoned his meanness, and acquiesced in his torture. That dream, then, of sharing, completing, finding in solitude on the beach an answer, was but a reflection in a mirror.

The signalled anthropormorphism in passages like this ("She saw . . . condoned . . . acquiesced") edges into sight our assumption of equivalence between inner and outer. In the passage describing the house left without people to observe it Virginia Woolf uses a neoclassical personification which strikes oddly, and which is intermelded with animal imagery. "It is a plain fact of consciousness that we think of a table or house as somehow existing independently of our perception of it," writes Stephen. Here, Virginia Woolf faces the problem of how we describe a house when it exists "independently of our perception of it." The answer in "Time Passes" is to see the object through time, and to use a discourse which points to human absence, sometimes with playful comfort as in the following passage, sometimes in mourning or ironic abruptness, as in those passages cut off within square brackets. ["A shell exploded. Twenty or thirty young men were blown up in France, among them Andrew Ramsay, whose death, mercifully was instantaneous."]

> Loveliness and stillness clasped hands in the bedroom, and among the shrouded jugs and sheeted chairs even the prying of the wind, and the soft nose of the clammy sea airs, rubbing, snuffling, iterating, and reiterating their questions—"Will you fade? Will you perish?"—scarcely disturbed the peace, the indifference, the air of pure integrity, as if the question they asked scarcely needed that they should answer: we remain.

The transposed, ludic quality of this passage is part of the decaying humanism of the concept "house"—an object constructed for human use and so now, without function, present only as lexical play. Beyond the ordinary house is the *lighthouse*, the furthest reach and limit of human concerns, an attempt to create a margin of safety before the sea's power becomes supreme.

The sound of the waves is heard throughout the book, sometimes louder, sometimes softer, but always there to remind us of the expanse of the world beyond the human, in the face of which all attempts at signifying and stabilising are both valiant and absurd. House and table are human objects, made to serve. Can the world of objects be made to sustain our need for signification, continuity, or permanence? These questions, brought to the fore by Hume's scepticism, and struggled with anew in the light of evolutionary theory by Stephen's generation, grind, like the dislimning sea, through *To the Lighthouse.*

The formlessness of the sea, the formed completeness of objects, challenge equally the authority of the human subject. "Subject and Object and the nature of reality" turns out not to be a vapid philosophical trope but the book's grounded enquiry, an enquiry which thrives through her father's concerns.

In generation, and in language, equally, (the making of children and of text) there is an attempt to ward off evanescence. In the course of her novel Virginia Woolf brings these desires within the surveillance of the reader. The tendency of the human to allow predominance to the human, to concur with our sense of our own centrality, is measured. Loading events and objects with symbolic weight comes to be seen as self-gratulation. So, as the work proceeds she emphasises momentariness and lightness. She empties and thins. The fullness of part 1 is replaced by the plainness of part 3. The work is filled with a sense of how ephemeral is human memory: bodies gone and minds with them. All substance is transitory.

In May 1925, as she was beginning *To the Lighthouse*, she wrote in her diary:

> This is going to be fairly short: to have father's character done complete in it; and mother's; and St. Ives and childhood; and all the usual things I try to put in—life, death etc. But the centre is father's character, sitting in a boat, reciting. We perish, each alone, while he crushes a dying mackerel—However I must refrain.
>
> (part 3)

In the completed work Mrs. Ramsay becomes characteristically the centre. The start of part 1 "The Window" as opposed to part 3 "The Lighthouse" imitates the self-doubting complexity of Mrs. Ramsay's sensibility, a fullness which is resolved later into others' simpler and more ideal memories of her. Certainly much of the emotional and artistic resourcefulness of the work goes into the making again, the repossession, of what the writer too soon had ceased to know: of Vita Sackville-West Virginia Woolf said in December 1925 that she "lavishes on me the maternal protection which, for some reason, is what I have always most wished from everyone." But the resourcefulness is also in composing what she could never have known: the meditative consciousness of the mother.

The sexual reserve of the writing is considerable. We never know the first names of Mr. or of Mrs. Ramsay. We do not accompany them to the greenhouses. The distance and decorum does not encourage the same knowingness in the reader as does our pleased recognition that the letter of the alphabet of philosophical knowledge that Mr. Ramsay cannot quite reach is that which begins his own name. Yet the Ramsays, the text assertively makes clear, are there when we are not. Their withdrawal emphasises substantiality and sexuality.

All signification relies on memory. In the language of the middle section of "Time Passes" there is a wilful element, a reclaiming, a making demands, by which the distributor of the language seeks to ward off the immersing sea, the elements, the air, the nonlinguistic world of human absence. The assertiveness, stylism, the hyperbole of linguistic desire, has parallels with that haunting figure, Grimm's fisherman's wife, whose story Mrs. Ramsay reads to James. And the grossness of the wife's demands have links also with the eagerness of the human to dominate the nonhuman.

> She read on: "Ah, wife," said the man, "why should we be king? I do not want to be king." "Well" said the wife, "if you won't be king, I will; go to the Flounder, for I will be king." . . . "And when he came to the sea, it was quite dark grey, and the water heaved up from below, and smelt putrid. Then he went and stood by it and said,
>
> "Flounder, flounder, in the sea,
> Come, I pray thee, here to me."

The last pages of the work void that final claim of the human on the world of process. They pare away symbol. The lighthouse itself when approached proves to be "a stark tower on a bare rock." The obsessional symbol-making urge of Mr. Ramsay, which is associated with his desire to clutch and hold on to experience, begins to ebb. In the fiction, despite his children's fears, he does *not* say "But I beneath a rougher sea" or "we perished, each alone," though in her diary she projected the scene with him "sitting in a boat, reciting We perish, each alone, while he crushes a dying mackerel."

Throughout the book Mr. Ramsay has raucously, anxiously, raised his voice against oblivion, terrified by death, and by that longer obliteration in which writing also is lost. But when they reach the place on their journey to the lighthouse where the boat sunk in the war (and in "Time Passes"),

> to their surprise all he said was "Ah" as if he thought to himself, But why make a fuss about that? Naturally men are drowned in a storm, but it is a perfectly straightforward affair, and the depths of the sea (he sprinkled the crumbs from his sandwich paper over them) are only water after all.

It is a poignant and comic moment. At the moment when highest mystification is expected we are offered complete demystification. His small gesture, in parenthesis, which recalls and then lets go of the parallel to dust to dust, ashes to ashes, is simply the sprinkling of crumbs on the sea, for the fishes.

That episode is immediately succeeded by another in which symbolism and the mystifying properties of human language and human gesture are relinquished. Lily, thinking their journey, imagines their arrival; " 'He has landed,' she said aloud. 'It is finished.' " The last words on the cross are half-conjured. Mr. Ramsay's journey and agony are momentarily, and uneasily, accorded a scale commensurate with his desires, though one on which, as readers, we are not obliged to dwell. The reference is fleetingly there. But it is immediately succeeded, and submerged, by Lily's finishing of her picture. The last words of the book are:

> With a sudden intensity, as if she saw it clear for a second, she drew a line there, in the centre. It was done; it was finished. Yes, she thought, laying down her brush in extreme fatigue, I have had my vision.

The change of tense, "it was done; it was finished," obliterates the earlier allusion. The scale of reference becomes immediate, and exact. The step is empty. The picture is finished.

The extraordinary serenity of the book, even while it includes desolation and harassment, depends upon its acceptance of attenuation. Loss, completion, ending, absence, are acknowledged. Evanescence is of the nature of experience, and although language can for a time make things survive, the work calmly rides out the anxieties of authorship. Though rhyme claims to outlive marble monuments, the pebble survives longer than Shakespeare. But people and language have lived. She renounces the grand, the symbolical, the enduring.

The moment is the moment of being alive in body and mind. In her diary in June 1927 she wrote: "Now one stable moment vanquishes chaos. But this I said in The Lighthouse. We have now sold, I think, 2555 copies" (part 3).

Lacan argues that symbol and the act of symbolisation represent the father. In freeing characters and text from the appetite for symbol Virginia Woolf may be seen as moving language and persons beyond subjection to patriarchy. And in doing so she transformed and absolved her own father through the act of writing. He comes back, but differently:

> I used to think of him and mother daily; but writing The Lighthouse, laid them in my mind. And now he comes back sometimes, but differently . . . He comes back now more as a contemporary. I must read him some day. I wonder if I can feel again, I hear his voice, I know this by heart?
>
> (part 3)

A conundrum remains: Virginia Woolf disclaims having "read" her father. Yet in this essay I have emphasised consonances between their written works. The answer may be that here she purposes a full reading, that act of intimacy, homage and appraisal in which we subject ourselves to a writer's complete work. She defers any such task, setting it in that warm never-never land of reading we hope "some day" to fulfill. The evasion persists. She must delay reading the father. Her earlier familiarity with his work had taken the form of dipping, scanning, listening, a flighty and intrigued resistance which allows rereading and pillaging and avoids immersion.

The wise act of writing in *To the Lighthouse* disperses parenthood and all its symbolic weight. Want and will give way, the want and the will of the fisherman's wife, of Lily Briscoe, of Mrs. Ramsay, Mr. Ramsay, of Cam and James. Subject ceases to dominate object. We are left with "the waves rolling and gambolling and slapping the rocks," "the frail blue shape which seemed like the vapour of something that had burned itself away," the line in Lily's picture which enters and holds "all its green and blues, its lines running up and across, its attempt at something." The line is at last freed from the referential. The picture can be completed.

The end of *To the Lighthouse* performs the experience of ending which has already happened in Mrs. Ramsay's reading aloud of Grimm's tale of The Fisherman's Wife. The end of a story allows annihilation and perpetuity at the same time. Things fall apart and—being written—for a time, endure.

So Mrs. Ramsay equably reads the apocalyptic conclusion to James:

> "Houses and trees toppled over, the mountains trembled, rocks rolled into the sea, the sky was pitch black, and it thundered and lightened, and the sea came in with black waves as high as church towers and mountains, and all with white foam on top."
>
> She turned the page; there were only a few lines more, so that she would finish the story, though it was past bedtime. It was getting late . . . It was growing quite dark.
>
> But she did not let her voice change in the least as she finished the story, and added, shutting the book, and speaking the last words as if she made them up herself, looking into James's eyes: "And there they are living still at this very time." "And that's the end," she said.

The elegiac triumph of the novel is to sustain entity. People survive when you are not there, when they are not there, in contradiction of Hume's assertion quoted at the beginning of this essay. ("Were all my perceptions remov'd by death . . . what is farther required to make me a perfect non-entity.") But they survive here in a kind of writing which eschews permanence. The last part of the book escapes from symbolic raising, placing its parental figures "on a level with ordinary existence," with the substance of a chair, a table, a house, with the depths of the sea which (as Mr. Ramsay at last thinks) are "only water after all."

Autonomy Theory

Frank Gloversmith

> *Whether we call it life or spirit, truth or reality, this, the essential thing, has moved off or on, and refuses to be contained any longer in such ill-fitting vestments as we provide.*
>
> "Modern Fiction," in *Collected Essays*

The polemical pieces increasingly represent her own criticism and fiction as exemplary of literary modernism, speaking for the revolutionary vanguard: *Modern Fiction* (1919), *Mr. Bennett and Mrs. Brown* (1924), *The Narrow Bridge of Art* (1927). Their sense of historical change authorizes this rejection of art that refuses to surrender outworn values, defunct meanings, sterile conventions. Though here, as with Scott and Austen, the interrelations of art, belief and the historical moment are simplified, Woolf displays shrewd insights into the complexities of style and literary form. The problems in artistic expression go well beyond definition in terms which are only artistic. Life, spirit, truth, reality: these universal concepts crop up throughout the polemics, as they do in her characters' thoughts. Woolf's own sense of their content is very much that of her own circle, naturally enough. Her philosophical supports are there in McTaggart, Moore, Fry, Charles Mauron; and they provide the base for her strictures on her older contemporaries. The novelist's task is anything but light; to see human beings not only in relation to one another, but in relation to the nature of reality as the modern mind now conceived it:

> Life is a luminous halo, a semi-transparent envelope surrounding us from the beginning of consciousness to the end. Is it not the

From *The Theory of Reading*, edited by Frank Gloversmith. Barnes & Noble Books, Totowa, New Jersey, 1984.

> task of the novelist to convey this varying, this unknown and uncircumscribed spirit . . . with as little of the alien and external as possible?

The elusive nature of the aberrant, complex consciousness is a notation from Freud, whose translations were being published by the Woolfs; the predominant images of mind and reality are transposed from Clive Bell's and Fry's own appraisals of modern art. Postimpressionism was the historic marker of the change in human nature and its understanding of itself which rendered established art and attitudes irrelevant. The "reality" of the Edwardians was inverted, it had become the alien, the external.

Inside the generalities, the sweeping phrases, the pronouncements and the fiats, the particular contradictions are very revealing. The plenitude of early novels is consonant with the richness and complexity of social values, attitudes, beliefs and behaviour. The narratives are grounded in their historical moment: the themes, the problems and the resolutions have a social authenticity. Part of the scornful dismissal of the Edwardians is that they write as if such authentication remained unchanged: they are obtuse to the major shifts in sociohistorical realities. But the substantiality of a Scott or Austen is also dismissed as alien and external: their strength is that they wrote poem-novels, formally compact. The Bennett and Wells fictions are not given such a reassessment, though even a Defoe can qualify. The updating of Austen, her installation as a modern lyrical novelist, is part of a need to provide Woolf's experimental forms with some support in the past. But it is also a sign of a deep unease about the consequences of accepting that any considerable narrative art can substantially incorporate social actions, beliefs, problems, practices, the stuff of daily living. Woolf strongly desires to formulate a comprehensive theory of narrative in which the concept of the aesthetic will necessarily, intrinsically, exclude sociohistorical material. The nervous, arrogant remarks about the carefully labelled "Edwardians," and about "ordinary everyday waking Arnold Bennett life," betray her sense of their nearness. Their concern with social problems, with class and money, with injustice, conflict and the possibilities of change, these all remain demanding and relevant, even if their artistic style and structures are old-fashioned.

Woolf impatiently reiterates her polemical slogan, "Life tells no stories." Popular novelists, in their bogus claims to follow tradition, seemed to do nothing else. Like E. M. Forster, she felt that all storytelling pandered to an atavistic sense. To carry on such narration in the 1910s and 1920s was anachronistic, since it ignored the nature and the recognitions of contemporary sensibility. The rigidities of fictive plotting precluded any awareness of contingency, indeterminacy, discontinuity, the elusive spirit of reality.

> If a writer were a free man, and not a slave, if he could write what he chose, not what he must, if he could base his work upon his own feeling, and not upon convention, there would be no plot, no comedy, no tragedy, no love interest or catastrophe in the accepted style.

(One free gesture would have been to alter the gender of all the pronouns here.) Woolf's minimal regard for received plotforms, for the genre-conventions, themes, patterns of development, is very effectively demonstrated in her fiction. The term "narrative" seems hardly to apply to her books, which strip action down to a few incidents, an even plane of meeting, drifting apart, being together at a meal or a party. The rhetorical emphasis of "No plot, no comedy" is programmatically realized. These dispersed, low-key and "sluggish" developments are not alternatives or variants of any other familiar narrative structures.

A novel, Woolf acidly exclaimed, was something she hoped not to be accused of any more—thinking of *Jacob's Room* as having reached, if not crossed, that shadow-line:

> The approach will be entirely different: no scaffolding; scarcely a brick to be seen; all crepuscular, but the heart, the passion, humour, everything as bring as fire in the mist.
>
> (*A Writer's Diary* [*hereafter referred to as WD*])

The experimental fiction is a rebuttal of realism, whose unquestioning "materialism" overloads the novel with fact, appearances, stolid characterization and labyrinthine plots. The answering structure can only be evoked in images, sensory, tactile, predominantly visual and painterly. The forms of modern perceptual reality are only to be alluded to obliquely, tentatively, impressionistically. So the critical terms must surrender claims to solidity, to conceptual definitiveness. Like the writing itself, they must take meaning from metaphor, from figurativeness, and evoke order and structure by poetic conceit. The Postimpressionist critical terminology was a crucial source of such concepts: luminosity, transparency, halo, mist, the crepuscular. Like "Pointillism" and "Impressionism," they may be indeterminate, loose, conceptually amorphous. But they mapped out Woolf's directions which, innovatory as they were, did not coincide with those of early modernism—James, Conrad—or of later modernism—Joyce, Lawrence, Stein.

The lyrical novel was Woolf's carefully crafted, scrupulously considered form, subjected to experiment and supported by critical research. The theoretical terms were part of the provisionality, and the experimental pieces and the novels themselves were always controlled by the theory. For Woolf, the fiction confirmed the original conceptions. They brought together her sense that form itself is a perception of relations independent of detail and appearance; that a writer's vision suffuses the whole writing with a fierce yet impersonal presence; and that imagery, metaphor and symbol can unify the composition. Her fundamental project, which made explanations so difficult, was to refashion the medium itself, to reshape its every detail. The restrictions of realistic plot were only a signal of the inadequacy of prose itself. The lyrical novel is to be the novel-poem, not only closely structured like a sonnet, but using its rhythms, its phrasing, its patterns, its density of language. Woolf's theory assumes a total distinction between prose and poetry; and, very selectively, considers lyrical intensity to be the quintessential quality of poetry itself. She was not concerned to make fiction less prosaic, nor to add metaphoric patterns or symbolic focus to a basically expressive narrative language. The fiction is to be a poem, not to be just poetic. The experiment is extreme, like the theory; the ambition and the accomplishment are audacious.

Woolf's astounding attempt was to make everything structural, to make each and every word contribute to the form—perhaps only feasible, if even then, in a sonnet or a brief lyric. This is her form of what she sensed in the poetic language of the Brontës, "an untamed ferocity perpetually at war with the accepted order of things." Her key-term for this is, aptly enough, "saturation": it comprises word-choice, fluent phrasing, echoic sentences, a patterning of syntax, a rhythmic disposition of longer paragraphs, a reptition of key-words, the use of images and literary allusion. The whole passage of Clarissa's sewing by the window is set out by Sean O'Faolain [in *The Vanishing Hero*] as vers libre: "Quiet descended on her, calm, content . . . listens to the passing bee" (*Mrs. Dalloway* [hereafter referred to as *MD*]). This is just as easily seen in the section in which Septimus responds to the livingness of the trees (*MD*). (The whole of Septimus's reverie without verbal changes, has been incorporated in an English version of *Noh* drama, *The Green Park*, by Richard Taylor. Even the attempt at a Bennett-Galsworthy type of writing, *The Years* (1937), is unable to shake off this kind of movement:

> The quick northern river come down from the moors;
> It was never smooth and green,
> Never deep and placid like southern rivers.
> It raced; it hurried.
> It splayed itself, red, yellow and clear brown,
> Over the pebbles on the bed . . . .
> She watched it eddy round the arches;

> She watched it make diamonds and sharp arrow streaks
> Over the stones.

The final novel, *Between the Acts* (1941), originally included poems in metre; and throughout the book, Isabella's inner-monologue ("musing," "humming," "muttering") is represented by this lyrical notation:

> Dispersed are we. The wave is broken.
> Left us stranded, high and dry. Single,
> separate on the shingle. Broken is the
> three-fold ply . . . . Now I follow . . . . To what
> dark centre of the unvisited earth, or wind—
> brushed forest, shall we go now? Or spin
> from star to star and dance in the maze of
> the moon? Or?

Nothing suggests that this is satiric in intent, and certainly not that it makes fun of Woolf's own style, as she had so extensively developed it throughout *The Waves*. Other figures in the book, like Bart and his sister Mrs. Swithin, speak to each other exclusively through quotations, poetic allusions and verbal jingles.

Two writers were singled out as her models for lyrical prose: Sterne and De Quincey. The lines from Sterne are pleasant, fluent, visually fresh, musical; Woolf clearly aims at such effects. Discussing De Quincey, she concludes that a writer is poetic in "gathering up and putting together these echoes and fragments," to "arrive at the true nature of an experience." This sums up her strategy for getting rid of the realistic novel's massive narrative blocks: the marginal and contingent details, in their textural density, will create a finer sense of perceptual reality. The "central things," the major truths about living must submit "to beautification in language" (*WD*). She faces the difficulty of doing without the major structural patterns, the narrative strategies, the usual modes of action and characterization. She acutely senses the danger of making her language both too fluid and too atomized, verbally fragmented: "One must write from deep feeling . . . . And do I? Or do I fabricate with words, loving them as I do?" (*WD*). This "pendulum" principle, swinging from "the generalization of romantic poetry" to particularization, was also a procedure that risked colouring everything with the writer's own perceptions. She felt the accuracy of Fry's warning that she was overdoing the prose-lyric vein: "I poetise my inanimate scenes; stress my personality; don't let the meaning emerge from the matière." But her determination to convert the novel into completely expressive prose remained throughout. The selected guardians—Sterne, Peacock, De Quincey, Proust—made her feel that good novelists are poets insofar as they write "for the sake of the beauty of the sentence, and not for the sake of its use." Her revision of *The Waves* is directed by this thought: "to break up, dig deep, make prose move as prose has never moved before: from the chuckle, the babble, to the rhapsody" (*WD*).

Most criticism has shown positive appreciation of Woolf's search for alternative large-scale modes to give the novels a clear structure. The verbal music prompted E. M. Forster's description of her form as characteristically that of the sonata, instancing the three movements of *To the Lighthouse*. This analogy is pressed home by E. K. Brown, analyzing the development and musical interweaving of themes: part 1 hymns the splendour of life (with some actual chanting and singing by characters); part 2 is a "sombre lamentation"; part 3, a symphonic finale, blends the two earlier sections, and closes with "great chorus." The mixed configurations—sonata, symphony, hymns, chants, chords—like that of "a formal dance" (J. Bennett)—are so nebulous that they only emphasize the difficulty of discerning clear outlines. There are comparable drawbacks with many related suggestions: the three sections are the three lighthouse beams (Fleishman); the lighthouse is a multifaceted symbol (Tindall); each book is a web of interconnected images (Brower, Hartman). The unity and coherence is attributed to a network of motifs, metaphors and symbols, but these are often inseparable from the "local texture" of reiterated figures. The discussion of full-scale patterning dissolves into analysis of "verbal nuances," and finally into the reader's "hazy, synaesthetic impression," as repetition becomes disintegrative and monotonous (Lodge). The critical goodwill in all these figurative labellings is in their wish to stress the forward impetus, the thrust and movement. The more convincing analyses show such impetus is present, not in separable features like images, but in the movement of the language itself. It has a simultaneous flow and acceleration, and a pausing rhythm (Hartman). This has been brilliantly analysed (Mepham, 1976) as a sustained stimulation of the reader's physical enactment of the text's "bodily" action, its compelling—in enunciation, in breathing, in syntactical phrasing—a physical reception which determines the imaginative comprehension. But the force of this analysis is to show how thoroughly Woolf did saturate every minuscule part and item of her language. The extensive, complex elements are composed of innumerable units and functions. The holistic, unifying principles are abstract, metatextual. "There are the oppositions between life and death, presence and absence, sterility and fertility . . . creating unity out of disorder."

Woolf's own frequent use of visual and spatial figures to describe her methods and her forms only stresses how elusive the temporal rhythms are.

The Fry—Mauron terminology of volumes and of montage is only the most obvious. Discussions with the painter Jacques Raverat produce similar ideas: the novel as composition, as sketch, as concentric circles, as diagram. She imagines a new novel: "I shall have two different currents—the moth flying along; the flower upright in the centre." This is part of her notebook musings when she stops "to consider the whole effect." Much of this is a principled resistance to the relentlessly chronological calibration of novelistic plot, with its keyboard precision and its alphabetic logic of conflict, crisis and resolution. The linearity of plot was one-directional, a railway-line, besides engendering much cumbersome description. Spatial metaphors suggested the multiplexity of experience, the simultaneity and coexistence of contrary impulses and ideas, the copresence of past and present, of the personal and the impersonal. The most compelling of the explicit, large-scale figures are spatiotemporal, a complex imbrication of movement and arrest. So the lighthouse's altering beams of light and intervals of darkness; the triple motion of waves-gathering, equipoise, dispersal; the movements of the sun during a whole day, with the intermittence of darkness. There are long-term contrasts of outside motion and flux with inside stillness and harmony: city traffic against private rooms (*MD*, The Waves [hereafter referred to as *W*]); wind, storm, and sea, against quiet gatherings of friends (*To the Lighthouse* [hereafter abbreviated as *TL*], *W*, *The Years* [hereafter referred to as *Y*]).

Woolf's project was "to tell all . . . everything, everything," and to tell it in a "playpoem," an "Elegy," a "novel about Nothing." This apparently ineffable form and substance—"everything I know"—has given literary criticism its two Woolfs: the Mystic and the Psychologist. The same elements in her writing illustrate each analysis: the connections between Septimus and Clarissa, and the closing metaphors about "redemption"; Mrs Ramsay's becoming "a wedge-shaped core of darkness," and her "return" after death; the intuitive reading of one another's thoughts by a whole group in *The Waves*; the frequent occurrence of trancelike "Moments." So many points in the fictions are interpreted as images of transcendence, or as images of psychic penetration, even as both at once. Climaxes are very often in terms of rising or sinking, climbing or falling, ascending or descending. But they all seem to be held within one form or another of the narrative's unfailing activity: *looking*. The authentic self, the clear mind, is "a central oyster of perceptiveness, an enormous eye." The flux of life, boisterous or momentarily stilled, is watched from a window: Woolf herself (*Room of One's Own*), the lady writer (*W*), Elizabeth on a bus (*MD*), Mrs Ramsay; or dangerously thrilling, surveyed from the roadside: Woolf again ("Street Haunting"), Clarissa, and Eleanor (*Y*). The regard of many separate figures may focus on an external point: a car, a plane (*MD*); the lighthouse; the sea (*TL*, *W*). Or the regard of all will turn to one person, present or absent: (Clarissa, Mrs Ramsay, Jacob, Percival (*W*).

> For the eye has this strange property: it rests only on beauty; like a butterfly it seeks colour and basks in warmth. . . . The eye is sportive and generous; it creates, it adorns; it enhances.

This concept of the *regard* is the prime token of Woolf's "everything," her psychology and philosophy, the "silence" that the playpoem is to articulate. Perception and the perceptual reality are the ubiquitous, singular and obsessive concerns, determining every level of the writing. They are humanly inextricable, mutually defining: the flux of being and the flow of awareness produce and sustain each other. The beauty is there for the eye to rest on; but it, in turn, only exists by creating and enhancing:

> Examine for a moment an ordinary mind on an ordinary day. The mind receives a myriad impressions—trivial, fantastic, evanescent, or engraved with the sharpness of steel. From all sides they come, an incessant shower of innumerable atoms; and as they fall, as they shape themselves into the life of Monday or Tuesday, the accent falls differently.

This radical relocation of the novelist's interest, "an ordinary mind on an ordinary day," affects every feature of the representation. The uninterrupted flow of awareness must prompt an uninterrupted flow of words to ensure the motions of the real:

> An immense profusion of sensations, images, sentiments, memories, impulses, little larval actions that no inner language can convey, that jostle one another on the threshold of consciousness, gather together in compact groups, loom up all of a sudden, then immediately fall apart, combine otherwise and reappear in new forms.

Nathalie Sarraute, in describing this identity in Woolf's writing of the form and the content, precisely defines its distinctive processual nature. The narrative "propones"—Sarraute's term—opens laterally, incorporates a circularity, while it never interrupts it own forward motion. Sarraute's neologism for this form, "tropism," distinguishes its aims from the "inner language" of modern psychologistic writing, since it essentially binds outer and inner. It catches the conflicting, shifting contingencies which conform briefly, to be replaced by the next conformation. (One concealed metaphor in Sarraute's account is Woolf's own favourite symbolic emblem, that of waves). Intermittency, the distintegration into the random, is that feature of the perceived and of the perception that insistently prompts the human ordering, just as it insistently threatens it.

The abstract motions of the narrative, linking its multiplying tropisms, are those of the aesthetic theories which Woolf developed from Fry, Mauron and G. E. Moore. The abstraction includes what is comprehended as "seeing," for "the central oyster of perceptiveness, an enormous eye," is the aesthetic sensibility. It is that other sense of "vision," that rapt intransitive attention which intuitively grasps harmony and relations. What a character here sees is little or nothing to do with the optical:

> The carriages, motor-cars, omnibuses, vans, sandwich men . . . some aeroplane overhead was what she loved; life; London; this moment of June.
>
> (*MD*)

> It was odd, she thought, how if one was alone, one leant to things, inanimate things: trees, streams, flowers; felt they expressed one; felt they became one.
>
> (*TL*)

> Snow falling—a sunflower with a crack in it; the yellow omnibus trotting along the Bayswater Road.
>
> (*Y*)

> Then (as I was walking in Russell Square last night) I see the mountains in the sky; the great clouds; and the moon which is risen over Persia. I have a great and astonishing sense of something there which is "it."
>
> (*WD*)

> The idea of some continuous stream, not solely of human thought, but of the ship, the night . . . all flowing together: intersected by the arrival of the bright moths. A man and a woman are sitting at the table talking.
>
> (*WD*)

Each "moment" is the realization of a unity, an interconnection between all things; the perceiver's "state of mind" is the rapt intransitive attention of the aesthetic sensibility. The harmony is in the relation itself, the design as index of all design, of universal coherence. The implications are mystical only insofar as Woolf has made a total and absolute value, a textual metaphysic, of the psychology of perception and the theory of aesthetic feeling developed by Fry and Moore. So the individual components are fortuitously specific, their particularity swept into a patterning which is nonspecific, abstract, idealist. The omnibuses and vans are interchangeable with the trees and streams, and these again with the clouds or the moths. Essentially, the units dissolve in the flux, outer and inner: there is an equalization of everything "seen." The omnibus, the snow, London, life, are essentially just as abstract and just as particular as one another. The perception of their relations overrides their differentiation: abstract or concrete, outer or inner, each component has an identical status and function. The perceiver, whether an internal character, or an actual person (Woolf in Russell Square), or the novelist (Woolf planning *The Moths*) "is aware of 'life itself'; of the atmosphere of the table rather than of the table; of the silence rather than of the sound." (Woolf's comment on the writing she most learnt from, that of Dorothy Richardson.)

"Her discoveries are concerned with states of being and not with states of doing": what is singled out in Richardson is also clearly Woolf's own project. The "trophies brought to the surface," which other writers have "guiltily suppressed" are those which Sarraute describes. Despite the Freudian hints, the retrievals are not from the deep unconscious, the regions of libidinal or visceral response. Joyce's explorations were profoundly shocking to her: "The pages reeled with indecency . . . This goes back to a pre-historic world" (*WD*). "How distressing, how egotistic, insistent, raw, striking, and ultimately nauseating" (*WD*). The intensities of the moment of perception have no deep, tentacular roots, no reaching after the inarticulable and prereflective grounds of unmediated experience. That they can seem so, as for instance with Mrs Ramsay's becoming "a wedge-shaped core of darkness," is an effect of their being context-free. Just as the components of the moment are interchangeably physical objects, places, ideas, whose differential qualities are pared away; just so the state of mind is unmotivated, disjoined from any immediate causal ground. But Mrs Ramsay attains no private psychic revelation; the reader is given no subtle personal psychological insights. This moment is like many others, not only her own, but those of other characters, in this and in other novels by Woolf.

The crucial turns and narrative climaxes are the representations of states-of-mind, impersonal and interchangeable in their contouring. They are not specific or restricted to the context, not given dramatic motivation. The state-of-mind is not definable as the consequence of sense response, since the objects and places are not given full-bodied sensuous identity. Neither is it built up from thought processes, from mental response to the provacation of action and immediate pressures. Woolf's characters, as thinking and feeling subjects, are not versions of the relativized consciousnesses of modernistic fiction. The trans-individual awareness that connects all the figures in *The Waves*, or relates Clarissa, Walsh and Septimus in *Mrs. Dalloway*, is necessarily contrary to such psychological differentiation. What each figure may attain is an access to a perceptual real which could not be self-identical if it varied from one sensibility to another. The perceptual real, caught by the contingent, transitory moment, is the persisting horizon of the narrative itself. The narrative is a continuous representation and dramatic enactment of a mode of consciousness which is only intermittently coincident with that of internal figures. The preferred consciousness will reflect this narrative mode, and be attributed with the same power to build fictions of unity. Clarissa and Mrs Ramsay set out to bring together the others who are scattered and isolated: this social harmonizing will be a party, a luncheon, a holiday group, a reunion of friends, even match-making for the young. Each is a form of the creative moment, a shared state of being, an aesthetic patterning of human relationship.

> This, that, and the other; herself and Charles Tansley and the breaking wave; Mrs Ramsay bringing them together; Mrs Ramsay saying 'Life stand still here'; Mrs Ramsay making of the moment something permanent (as in another sphere Lily herself tried to make of the moment something permanent).
>
> (*TL*)

The blunt reminder in parenthesis is superfluous, since all the texts are constructed on these parallels between various forms of aesthetic sensibility. The society hostess, the mother, the painter, poet or writer: each manifest its predominance, its definitive human centrality.

It is this would-be absoluteness, this dogmatic comprehensiveness, which fractures the narratives and which makes them much richer texts than they would have been, had they mainly illustrated the theoretical notions from which Woolf begins. The aesthetic sensibility, whether intuitively receptive or actively creating harmony, is tested by the autonomy of the "moment." As a moment of ordered perception, it readily falls back into the assembled constituents: if the trees can be yellow omnibuses, then no ordering or selection has been achieved. As Katherine Mansfield remarked: "Everything being of equal importance, it is impossible that everything should not be of equal unimportance." Again, if the trees are there insofar as "they express one"—Clarissa, Septimus, Mrs Ramsay, Susan (in *The Waves*)—then no relation or connection is really being made outside the perceiving ego. Clarissa's apocalyptic realization of her final identity with Septimus is literally that: a relation to a version of her self. The climactic evening party, to which the whole narrative leads, is effectively not shown in itself. That parallel sequence, the Ramsays' dinner-party, is an intriguingly complex instance of the extended "moment," and its self-deconstruction. The disparates are said to be reconciled, and social communion rendered as poetry and music, or even as a transcendent, sacred communion. Yet Woolf's own language insists on the scene as visually, graphically rendered, on the deliberate, individual ordering by one character, and on the way everything is "composed." The poignancy is in the rendering of the fragility, in the separateness of Mrs Ramsay's view, and in the disintegration of the scene as she leaves:

> She waited a moment longer in a scene which was vanishing even as she looked . . . it had become, she knew, giving one last look at it over her shoulder, already the past.

The exhilaration of a Clarissa, the affirmations of a Mrs Ramsay, the ecstatic perceptions of a Jinny, a Bernard or a Rhoda (*W*) share a high-pitched breathlessness which hardly restrains its anxieties and hysteria. The states-of-mind and states-of-being, even if they are shareable, admit their impotence "against that fluidity out there" (*TL*).

This fracturing of the autonomy of the individual state-of-mind and of the communal state-of-being is given other contradictory and sombre forms. Clarissa's buoyancy and self-discipline, her defiant affirmations of significant order have an inner contouring of depression, disintegration of the self, and explicit traumatic intuitions of absurdity and incoherence. Existence is simultaneously the one (Clarissa) and the other (Septimus): they are not contrasts, alternatives, or mutually exclusive. The "madness," as E. M. Forster noted, is always lucidly, rationally presented. The teasing ambivalence is in the way that the discourse of "madness" is an extreme extension of Clarissa's (and the narrative's) mode of awareness. Septimus is locked in an infinity of moments, condemned to an endless hyper-awareness. This is touched on for all the figures in *The Waves*, and given a singularly intense form in the presentation of Rhoda. The narrative seems to include representations of the destructive cost of its own values, especially its distinctive mode of consciousness. This is one of the troubled impulses which inform the extended midsection of *To the Lighthouse*, "Time Passes." This "narrates the production of a discourse of madness." It is, paradoxically, an aesthetic ordering, by Woolf, of the destructiveness consequent on the attempt to comprehend (i.e. to aesthetically order) the flux of perceptual reality. Time, place, person are annihilated: the lyrical, rhythmic language is to image that annulment. It strives to represent an unmediated, inhuman reality; and obscurely admits what it would strenuously deny, that it is self-mirroring. The aesthetic sensibility here faces that chosen definition of itself, and its consequent disintegration. The bad infinity cannot be authenticated as an objective, nonhuman flux. To attempt to authenticate it is only to point within, to describe the perceiver's chosen form of perception.

Woolf was always keenly aware of the related problems of authority, narrative control and personal inflections in prose. She detested the masculine reiteration of "I . . . I . . . I" in fiction, and felt that to "lyricize the argument" would help avoid this. Reading Joyce and Richardson brought out strongly the way that any notation of consciousness set traps for the "damned egotistical self." The rejection of plot and the strategies of realism increased the dangers of her fluency: "I have come to a crisis in the matter of style. It is now so fluent and fluid that it runs through the mind like water. . . . Shall I now check and consolidate?" (*WD*). The piquancy is that her major concern is the fluency of the sensibility: to set this at a distance would be to question, to qualify, to ironize. This is the source of the narrative checks and consolidations in the richly diverse characterization and language of James, Conrad and Joyce. Consciousness is conditioned, individualized, located by contrasts in their fictions. Woolf represents consciousness as unconditioned and transindividual: and the authentication for its being so must inevitably be her own consciousness, the sensibility that saturates the text. The cross-play of contrasting minds is the source of tension and drama in any modern fiction which has undercut the predominance of outer action. But the centres of consciousness that encircle Woolf's major figures only endorse the sensibility there represented. The contrast is with the obtuse, the impercipient, the buffoons of sensibility: Bradshaw, Holmes, Kilman; Tansley, Mr Ramsay (in part 1). They cannot be seen from the inside: Woolf's historiography of the consciousness sets them at the borders of nullity. The perception of a Walsh, a Tansley, even of a Mr Ramsay, is corrected or "redeemed" by its reverential assumption of the state-of-being incarnated in a Clarissa or in a Mrs Ramsay. Any irony in the text about the protagonists, explicit or unwitting, is about their incidental, diversionary preoccupations, mannerisms, personal behaviour. This is the dross that clogs the sensibility, the hindrances to the intuitive imagination. The six characters in *The Waves*, totally free of any irony, are never seen in any relation to that level of mundane involvement. Sensibility making total claims for itself cannot test them by ironic self-scrutiny, without modifying radically its fundamental assumptions: "When I write I am merely a sensibility. Sometimes I like being Virginia, but only when I'm scattered, and various and gregarious."

The history of the various versions of *The Moths* and its modulation into *The Waves*, confirms the accuracy of this rueful, ambivalent self-assessment. When the reviewers praised the novel's characters, she was genuinely puzzled, noting rather proudly that she meant to have none (*WD*). The ambiguities and the confusions about her own presence in the texts are reiterated throughout the *Diary*. "Who thinks it? And am I outside the thinker?" She worried that the books were "essays about myself," while developing a theory which could only maximize that possibility. *Jacob's Room* provides instances, with its miniessays about the mystery of personality, about perception, about the difficulty of writing fiction. The writer's appearance is meant to dramatize the difficulty of analysing or understanding character, a demonstration of Jacob's otherness and distance from the author. But her presence replaces his, blocks his becoming either mysterious or knowable. The more pervasive, less obvious presence, which perhaps marks all her novels, is in the close control of the representation. The sequences are manneristically patterned, the dialogue edited, the scenes restrained, the action minimalized. There is an arbitrariness which binds everything in to the author's originating conceptions about character, about action and about their representation. There is an open, ingenuous formulation of how this art of fiction involves the attribution to characters of qualities, intentions, and meanings which are validated only by their intrinsic interest:

> But something is always compelling one to hang vibrating . . . endowing Jacob Flanders with all sorts of qualities he had not at all . . . what remains is mostly a matter of guess work.

This power of fictive attribution is approvingly given to internal characters in other novels: Peter Walsh, Mrs Ramsay, Bernard. It is the whole point of *An Unwritten Novel* (1920). The *Diary* has many such reveries and speculations: "Street Haunting" demonstrates some of them. Most significantly, the whole argument of "Mr Bennett and Mrs Brown," a major illustration of her theory, depends on whose "attribution" of qualities to "Mrs Brown"—i.e., people, experience, life—is most convincing. The styles of the various attributions, of course, are in turn attributed by the winner herself, Virginia Woolf.

"Who thinks it? And am I outside the speaker?" Placing herself in view, directly in *Jacob's Room*, indirectly through Lily, Bernard, or Miss La Trobe, did not ensure her being outside the speaking. The "speaking" of the texts became increasingly idiosyncratic, multilayered, ambivalent in its origins and its narrative dispositions. Echoing her questioning, John Mepham asks "Who speaks in *To the Lighthouse*?" He brilliantly analyses the subtle modulations from the fictional subjects to the narration's own contribution. As Auerbach indicates, Woolf represents herself as "someone who doubts, wonders, hesitates," so that the fictive voice and the narrative voice are hardly distinguishable. This indeterminacy of attribution is used by Woolf "to provide extra dimensions of meaning and association on behalf of the subject." This is the author's addition of cross-reference, allusion and imagery which the internal figure "would recognize as expressive of the force and content of his (or her) experience." This single source of authentication, the character "itself," was Woolf's allegedly final authority in *Jacob's Room*. That Jacob or any other figure is part of the whole narration's flow of language is vital, however obvious, in this search for meaning's origins. That personality is mysterious, that identity is dislimned, is the founding perception of exactly this sort of narrative language. It is not a perception by the characters, but a conception about identity, which the figures serve to illustrate and embody. The slippage between fictive voice and narrative voice clearly works both ways: Woolf's mode of perception extends into that of the characters. The local strategies to keep the division flexible are the signals that it is there, and that it is being traversed. A minor example is the umbrella pronoun "One," which blurs and fuses the attitudes of character and of narrator, and often implicates the reader.

The rhetoric of the lyrical novel is not in the command of the characters: its generality and its structural function has to subsume their individuality. The metaphoric level, with its patterned systems of imagery and allusion, has formal functions that belong in most fiction to the plot. This innovatory displacement, at the centre of Woolf's experimentalism, was consciously at the expense of interest in characterization. The multidimensional play-poem moves on a vertical axis, a rhetorical, stylistic, verbal interaction. It discards the linear axis, the metonymic and syntagmatic procedures of expository narrative. What the characters say is of little or no importance, against how the saying is part of the totalizing, nonindividual movements of the language. The voice of the narration is composed by any and all other voices of characters, whose names are often irrelevant. Any page of *The Waves* can be quoted without names as an instance of the saturated texture and poetic movement that Woolf wanted. Such choric writing marks significant moments in all the novels, even in the would-be factual *The Years* (e.g., the conversation between Sarah and North, "Present Day"). The intonations that bind the separate utterances together are almost always in the spectrum from the poignancy of recollection, the commemorative, to the plangently elegiac:

> "Well, we must wait for the future to show."

"It's almost too dark to see."
"One can hardly tell which is the sea and which is the land."
"Do we leave the lights burning?"
One by one the lamps were all extinguished.

("Times Passes," *TL*)

The Waves is the most intensive and most extensive exploitation of every element contributing to the poem-novel. It elegantly displays how "lyricizing the argument" makes the writing choric in every part. The "argument" has disappeared, and the formality of the profuse figurative, rhythmic language has to provide its own contours and dramatic punctuation, its origins and its closures. The checks and consolidation of character and action have been abandoned. Language itself has to provide the objectification, the impersonality, the rein against the "damned egotistical self." But language is no more autonomous for these purposes than the states-of-mind which it is to express and to connect by its rhythms. This order of impersonality is not sealed into language as such, and certainly is not hermetically enclosed in imagery and metaphor. Woolf is obsessively concerned with style in language, which can only mean the decisions and choices she makes, explicitly or implicitly. The retreat to a hypothetical absolute position which language stripped of "personality" should have is illusory, like "omniscient perspective" attributed to metaphoric patterning in the lyrical novel. (Itself a pseudogenre: compare R. Freedman.)

The distinctively individual, even idiosyncratic, deployment of language, verbally and structurally, is enthusiastically appraised by Woolf's critics. The further assumption is that the metaphoric profusion brings impersonal, objective reference through the archetypal force of its patterns: sun, sea, light and dark, day and night, the seasons, gestation, the life span, the flux of nature or of human consciousness. Again, however, these can only be present in specific conceptions and formulations. Their presence in the flow of language that composes the prose-poem here carries, necessarily, many traces of their earlier formulations. These are, by Woolf's studied choices, increasingly confined to their use in earlier English verse. (She has an indifference, even a strong aversion, to modern poetry.) Her prose, then, has its affiliations not with other prose, and not with traditional fiction—except when she interprets particular instances as lyrical novels. The language is "poeticized," but, again, in relation to a specific interpretative conception of poetic tradition. This singles out the quintessentially melodic, the rhythmic and the free-flowing, the insistently metaphoric, the sensuously impressionistic, the verbally "orchestrated." It ignores the play of ideas in verse, the referential, the nonevocative relational elements, the dramatic representations of conflict with the self or with the world. This highly selective definition of the poetic comes from a search for the resonance and vibrancy of words disjoined from specific contexts, persons, perceptions, or dramatic situations. The "poetic" is shorthand for reflection and reverie circling around abstractions labelled "life," "Time," "Death," extrapolated from literary sources, and set out as the mythic forms which control the rhythms of the aesthetic sensibility.

A characteristically revealing note on the genesis and the intention of her writing is apropos of the midsection of *To the Lighthouse* (*WD*). She remarks that it is incredibly abstract, "all eyeless and featureless with nothing to cling to." At the same instant, she is struck by her exhilarated fluency, a rushing and "scattering" of language. "Why am I so flown and apparently free to do exactly what I like?" Not only are scene and characters removed, there is to be no narrator or implied author. This withdrawal of agency or focus is the enabling of the poetic narrative itself, the occasion for the voice of language to speak. But the annulment or death of this author allows the release of other authors. The style which aims at writing degree zero lets in all the other styles, and the passage is a pastiche of a whole range of idioms and tones. They include the Biblical, the prophetic, the elegiac, the stoically philosophical, the grotesquely comic, the visionary and apocalyptic. Specific borrowings might be traced to the Authorized Version, seventeenth-century baroque prose, Pater, Arnold, Dickens and Hardy. The images indeed have "nothing to cling to," no house, no people, no situation. The voices become a medley of disparate voices whose only combinatory source has to be this narrator. Otherwise the words fall back into the myriad of atomistic sensations which present themselves for unification, for lyrical "orchestration," by one voice. Woolf has to mediate, she cannot disappear behind language; she remains as a separate, authenticating presence, all the more pervasively because she has deconstructed the alternative mediations. The flux here is a stream of consciousness, but not that of a "nature" or of the language: "It is finally the emancipated associative flow of the novelist herself."

A variation of this inference about narrative form and its authority, the sense of "Who speaks?" in this writing, produces the related suggestions that the one developed character is the androgynous mind (Hartman, 1975); or the feminine sensibility (Spivak, 1980). Both ideas, much discussed by feminists, have considerable support in Woolf's own criticism. They restore the possibility that the autonomy of the lyrical novel could dramatize the distance between the fictive voice (singular or composite) and the narrative voice. But their consonance, their interweaving, and their ultimate singleness are evinced in the peculiar form that Woolf gives to the internal monologues.

The "moments" and states-of-mind are always expressed as interior monologues; and the whole of *The Waves* consists of interrelated lyrical soliloquies. However, they have been edited, effectively shorn of all the features associated with theatrical soliloquy, or the complementary dramatic monologue. Whatever the variations, these traditional forms are utterances in which the speaker shows a sense of being situated. There is a sense of provocation, of opposition, of likely (or silently voiced) answers, which are anticipated, summed up, reflected on. They are theatrical or "dramatic" in that they are located, with promptings and aftermath implied in the tense movements of the self-explanation and self-scrutiny. The soliloquy or monologue is an actual or mental withdrawal, but the thinker wants to act out all the implications of the actuality that informs the reflections. He addresses himself, and addresses others, temporarily absent; the soliloquizing is functional, directed, purposive.

The soliloquy or interior monologue in Woolf's fiction often signals its not being directed or purposively addressed. The ruefully reiterated "But to whom?" is disingenuous when it is not self-pitying. The language of the soliloquizer is not meant to communicate, to answer, to impinge. It is an intransitive address, a verbal composition, a metaphoric transcript of an elusive, self-validating intuition. Its separateness, its privacy, its radical otherness is precisely what the whole force of the writing privileges and authenticates. That fictive characters or the narrative's voice should attribute pathos or pain to this isolatedness is confused and confusing, even if this inflection is more valid than the first kind. This larger, encircling evaluation is, however, not allowed to bring this clash into the movements of the text. The lyrical fluency of expression is itself the obsessive iteration of continuity and undividedness. This continuum of words has a marked unity of tone, and is itself an extended monologue. It preserves its essential qualities by erasing dialogue, by suppressing possible answers, by curtailing its origin and provocation. The absence of direct verbal exchange is not a neutral obverse of the concern with mental or psychological interiors. The remarkably extensive use of indirect speech, the voice of the narrative filtering all other voices, is not another experimental feature, a value-free technique. Its obsessiveness bothered the novelist: "I think I can spin out all their entrails this way; but it is hopelessly undramatic. It is all in *oratio obliqua*. Not quite all; for I have a few direct sentences" (On *TL*, *WD*). Yet it is the oratio obliqua which gives the narratives their density, their pace and tone, their peculiar atmosphere and pitch, and provides the complex modes of control which impose form on the material. It is yet one more maniestation of the penetration into all the voices of the inflections of the narrative voice. The linguistic register is changed, not from one character to the next, nor from one kind of scene to another, but within the sentence. A rhetoric is provided which is meant to articulate impressions, thoughts and perceptions which are unrecognized by the fictive subject. The narrative "lends" its voice: but the voice it suppresses, however it might have fumbled its expression, cannot be heard. This stylistic variation of *erlebte rede*, then, may be seen as an ascription to nearly all the represented characters of fundamentally false consciousness.

The most obvious suppression of other discourse is seen in the peripheral dramatis personae. They are the gardeners, miners, cooks and cleaners, the street-singers and women with shopping bags. They are the "base-born," the "illiterate and underbred," the "veriest frumps," seen in a mass—"the mothers of Pimlico give suck to their young"—and as subhuman, animal-like—"crawling," with "stumps" for legs. (The delicately minded, old-fashioned, upper-middle-class periphrases signify the social origin of the suppression.) More significantly, there is omission of the complementary voice in the "dialogue" of friends, lovers, married couples. Richard Dalloway never speaks, yet is a paragon; the conversation of Clarissa and her passionate admirer Peter Walsh is transmogrified into a cluster of mock-heroic images; the marriage of true minds, the Ramsays', is distinguished by silences, when the indirect, smouldering resentments have been first released. The same pattern is used for Giles and Isa, the central married couple in *Between the Acts*. The validity of relationships is rarely expressed and rarely tested in the form of dramatic dialogue. Exchange, connection and confrontation are summarized by indirect report.

The clearest and most damaging suppression of dialogue is the denial of a voice to those agents in the action whose values and consciousness are antithetical to those of the protagonist. These are the buffoons who lack sensibility: but since their own discourse is not given, the ascription is self-confirming and shows up as allegation. Holmes, Bradshaw, Mrs Bradshaw, Whitbread, through omission, become caricatures; they do not exist on Clarissa's own plane. Equally with Tansley (*TL*) and Laycock (*Y*) or Mrs Manresa (*BA*): their attitudes and behaviour are already interpreted, and this bias turns out to be the attributed "humour" of the character. The sketchily presented Whitbread is constituted only from the idea that authority at its least unacceptable is bland, pompous, pedantic and self-satisfied. Bradshaw is similarly composed, but from a bitter hatred of arrogant authority, of its mindless, destructive imposition of order. The representation combines a quadrupled indirection with the fracturing of the narrative control. There are wild, savagely sarcastic passages on "Proportion" and "Conversion," an allegory of diabolism, which are unattributed and unascribable to any textual voice. The reader's sense that this might be "the most uncharming human being"—Lily's thought about Tansley, but it could be about Bradshaw or Doris Kilman—is not inferable from any instance of behaviour. The fiercely negative sentiments are so riddled with anxiety that they must stifle this hateful opposing voice, must perpetrate the same offence. This bizarre distortion of feeling, since it is approvingly installed in Clarissa's attitudes, refers the reader very directly back to Woolf as person, not as narrator or as implicit author, but simply as the explicit, judging writer. (The same disruption occurs often in the work of E. M. Forster.)

There is evident in all these texts a full-scale "dialogue" between male and female, masculine and feminine. Their bold and damagingly simple lines have often been tabulated: Intellect/Intuition, Fact/Vision, Words/Silence, Society/Solitude, Clock-time/Duration in consciousness, Realism/Impressionism. *To the Lighthouse* has the clearest, most complete enactment of the antithesis. Its clarity and strength, however, do not consist in its giving equal presence to the complementary or adversative types of consciousness. Mr Ramsay's inflexibly linear mind, immersed in externalities, is perceived through the intuitive feminine consciousness, which pervades all the writing, though it centres itself in Mrs Ramsay. The masculine mode of a Bradshaw is here temperately imaged, indulged with wry mock-heroic imagery which denies him any direct voice or presence. He is only immediate when he contemplates the wonder of Mrs Ramsay's being. The tilt in presentation, the uncontested nature of Mrs Ramsay's "triumphs" and "trophies," means that the narrative's own ultimate values are less securely dramatized. The intuitive and visionary sensibility is attributed to the "feminine" mode of consciousness, in turn identified with that of the artist. Lily, the painter/writer, may be internal, and her "canvas" finally disposable. But the text itself, which validates their shared sensibility, demonstrates its aesthetic mode, again without proving it in confrontation with the antagonistic "masculine" mode. The ultimate appeal is to the aesthetic visionary mode, this novel itself, which is the controlled comprehension of all else.

The masculine/feminine polarity crosses gender lines: despite her name, Kilman, this character is evoked as "masculine" in her wilfulness. Jacob and Septimus, destroyed by the men's world, are "feminine" in temperament; as are all the artists and writers, like Bernard, Neville and Louis—three of the four clustered together in *The Waves*. This polarity of principles, taken as ironized by Woolf, and resolved (as "androgyny") or superseded, is itself part of a larger dialogue. It is part of the narrative politics in which the displacement of realism is part of the re-ordering of experience by her own aesthetic forms: "If Woolf moves away from facts and crises it is because she denies the claim of such ordering to be all-inclusive" (Beer, 1979). The railway-line of Ramsay's logical progress is that of realistic narrative, of male ideology and philosophy, and the brutal, destructive hegemonic social order. The lateral, associative movement of Woolf's writing then symbolizes the receptivity to other possibilities and movements, alternative modes of social living. This intentionality may well be perceived; but the caricatural onslaught and the suppression of the masculine voices are not only tactical, a means of temporarily suspending their authority. As the uncontrolled feeling indicates, there is a fundamental ambiguity, a hyperdefensiveness about the writing whenever the Bradshaw-mentality is arraigned. The affected serenity of the witty allegorical conceits—Proportion, Conversion, the Seven Deadly Sins in a mackintosh (Kilman)—barely holds back a hatred for all interest in social ordering. This has been often mystified as a distaste for "the idea of Society as such." It is much more obviously an overanxious dislike of commitment, analysis, social change. It contains a vigorous rejection of the society in transition which she was observing, England between the wars. Her kind of "openness" to possible alternatives in social living, in the mid-1930s, is demonstrated very explicitly in *The Years*. The separate self, the centre, is the only location for change. Two of its proponents are given climactic, disruptive diatribes whose convolutions of ambiguous, unmotivated feeling refer straight back to the writer herself. All the bitterness of the earlier "exposures" of commitment is intensified in an unbalanced commentary on manifestoes, social concern, political activism. The "young man"—Leacock or Laycock—is given no speech: he is a textual space for this unlocated, unprovoked animus. The sad offence that is here to be inferred was in Doris Kilman's case a wish for other modes of social living, other ways of thinking, feeling, behaving. Kilman wants her own vocation, and wants to convince others about change. She must be a feminist, and the text darkly hints, probably a lesbian. But like the vituperated, silent male target here, she has to be convicted of the politics of envy. Social change and political commitment are only symptoms of the persistence of the deadly sin.

This imbalance and negativity of feeling is there in the overall structure of the books that confront the present as historical time. In *The Years*, Peggy's metaphysical ennui and North's onslaught on political activism are the contours of the whole section, "Present Day." The parellel closing section of *Between the Acts* echoes the sense of the present as vacillating, unsatisfactory. Both narratives elegiacally commemmorate the past, despite the intention to show its dead hand in the earlier novel. History and its processes are domesticated, privatized, and deconstructed into successive, atomistic "moments." In the last book, each age is encapsulated, by pastiche and light parody, as an aesthetic moment, abstracted, self-contained. The continuity between these moments is purely verbal, and tradition is intensely aestheticized. The chronology is lifted out of actual historical time, into the nonspecific phases of biological and evolutionary development. The pageant's history is, through the literary and the evolutionary filters, twice-removed from sociopolitical conflict or motivation, and from the causal-transformative mode of actual change. The present becomes a memory or a reliving of the past, and both dimensions, present and past, are not temporally rooted or specific.

This evacuating of the historical moment repeats what happens with each individual moment, that of the intuitive consciousness. Like the Ramsay's dinner-party communion among the disparate individuals, the moment elides into the past as it is registered—or because it is registered. Self-reflection and disintegration of what is observed coincide, often unwittingly, and at all levels. The myriad of sensuous impressions that are the spontaneous material of life itself, because of refraction through the prism of consciousness, break immediate sensation into its random components. Sensation itself, as a powerful unity, suffers dispersal, as the theory of unification through sensibility runs into its opposite. The impulse or apprehension cannot be sustained, unified with others, composing a fresh emotion or response towards the outside. There is a withdrawal, an evasion of immediacy and spontaneity: the composition of a moment halts the forward thrust: "Life stand still here!" The aesthetic alternative, making a work of art of the primary response, is intrinsically retrospective. What is occluded is openness, immersion, anticipation.

A favourite fantasy of Woolf's was that she would write a novel with all the fact on one page, and all the fiction on the facing page. *The Waves* came fairly close to realizing that project. "I shall do away with exact time and place. . . . My theory being that the actual event practically does not exist—nor time either" (*WD*). Behind the philosophical pretentiousness there is a complicated cluster of rejections, personal and social, which are triggered by tension, conflict, and confrontation. Terms like "event," "time," "proportion," "conversion" give a dignity and distance to responses which are far less measured and objectified. The hypostatizing of an aesthetic plane of "event" and "time," safely within the ambience of individual consciousness, complete the whole rationalization. Circumspectly absorbed by "feminine" comprehension, the "masculine" can be safely attributed with all the sources of disturbance impingeing on awareness. The demand of the other can be treated as alien, uncivilized, a threat to the self's centre. The "other," however, includes the self's emotions, desires, needs for connection. Seen as a threat to civility and equilibrium, such emotions are frenetically acted through in Clarissa's other self. Septimus vicariously acts out the nightmares of emotion, loss, destructive passions. The aesthetic sensibility, like Lily's and Mrs Ramsay's, must preserve its identity by refusing the turbulence of acceding to emotional tensions. Lily's "creativeness," her visionary sense, depend on stamping out her sexual response to Tansley, and on suppressing her insistently erotic awareness of Paul Rayley. The cost of individual, emotional autonomy is to kill off the "masculine" other which is within.

The suppression of the masculine discourse has more complicated motives than a principled opposition to an oppressive social ordering. But it is not a question of attributing it to personal, temperamental or embarrassingly intimate sources. The exclusion of emotions, which return in arbitrarily placed images of violence and eroticism, is a blanketing of ordinary daily living. The imaginary left-hand page of *The Waves* is inscribed with the six characters' daily lives—their work, their family origins, their relationships, their love-affairs and marriages, their interests and their behaviour. These are all the locations of conflict, tension, emotional interaction. The play-poem, the lyrical novel itself, represents their search for the perfected realm of perception, self-awareness, the unviolated sensibility. Here there is and must be total silence about work, family, daily behaviour. They pursue the good, the true, the beautiful, living itself apprehended as Significant Form. This pursuit pays its reluctant tributes to the value of what it must ignore, mostly in its agonizing sense of loss, isolation, anxiety and impotence. Their paradoxical defiance consists in seeing all these as signals of their especial distinction. But the crucial symbolic focus of the book, the ritual meetings to mark Percival's departure, then his early death, and later to commemorate his life, are the most ambivalent sequences in the whole of Woolf's writing. For Percival is no thinker, writer, or seeker after Platonic ideals. He never speaks, his consciousness cannot be entered: he has the unity and singleness of being that is marked by spontaneity in action. The characters' sad ceremonials are their shared longing to know and to be Percival, to live the life that has been silently signalling from the imaginary other pages.

Panel Discussion

Gillian Beer (Chair), Bernard Bergonzi,
John Harvey, Iris Murdoch
[hereafter referred to as GB, BB, JH, and IM, respectively]

GB: I thought we might start by asking each of the three panelists how they find the presence of Virginia Woolf in their own practice as novelists. Is she somebody who can now simply be bypassed? Or is she still a recalcitrant being, a recalcitrant *writing*, which needs to be circumvented, written through, obliterated, transcribed? I'll start by asking Bernard Bergonzi.

BB: What's the question, Gillian?

GB: Do you still *need* Virginia Woolf, or can you do without her? [laughter]

BB: Well I *did* without her for a long while, I think. That is to say, I read her, a number of her books, when I was quite young—about nineteen or twenty. And then there was a great occlusion of her reputation in the fifties, and she seemed to have pretty well sunk without trace. What is interesting is the way the reputation has come up again so much in the last twenty years, hence this well-attended Centenary Conference.

I suppose I went back to her texts for professional reasons: I found myself lecturing on her, every year on *To the Lighthouse*—a book which I really came to admire through the process of teaching it. I think we're all familiar with that activity—how books which you take up as a chore, because you have to, you can actually come to respect and admire. Of course it can go the other way too, alas. But I think probably my dealings with Mrs Woolf have been of that critical and professional kind. Insofar as I have written a bit of fiction myself, I don't think there was any presence of Virginia Woolf in it or near it; the sources of that were quite other.

JH: I should likewise say that I hadn't, before writing myself, enormously read or drawn on Virginia Woolf, though over the years I have been reading and enjoying her. I should say also, that what I find myself enjoying more and more *is* the writing, and the variety of the writing—including the criticism, and some of the Memoirs, especially the "Sketch of the Past." Of the fiction, the novel which I do go back to again and again is the one that I suppose everyone does, *To the Lighthouse*.

How one might nowadays be influenced by it I don't know. One returns to it I think chiefly to appreciate the art with which it arranges and focusses the family experience that it is based in. It does seem to me almost *the* exemplary novel about a father. I know that Mr Ramsay isn't to be assimilated entirely to Leslie Stephen; that Virginia Woolf leaves out his main achievements and a number of his good qualities, and exaggerates other features of him and some of those exaggerated features seem to be ones where his character especially overlaps with hers. One gathers that the anxiety about whether or not he's a failure, with its constant, exorbitant demands for reassurance and support, and for constant encouragement, was something which was marked in her as well as in him. And I'd have thought that for various reasons one would feel that the novel is not exactly a portrait of—or doesn't even try to be portrait of—the real person that her father was. But it *is* a portrait of, as it were, the daimon of her father that she's nurtured inside herself over the years, which needs to be, in a way, exorcised, *negotiated* especially. And it seems to me that what she does in the novel is to negotiate that partly invented image of her father, about which she has intense, varied feelings, about which she's divided, seeking really a right order for the memories of him, or the images of him, which her imagination gives her.

I prefer the word "order" to "structure" because I think the right order is both the right structure and the right sequence. The novel is a sequence, and one can see that it has worked as a sequence in bringing her to the right attitude in the way that, along with the predominantly malign images that you have in the early parts of the novel, she increasingly finds a place for *benign* images of him. As, for instance, when the boat has been becalmed and all the bad passions of the family seem to be about to burst out; and then the wind fills the sails and takes the boat forward, without any of the explosions from Ramsay that have been expected, but instead, simply with his mysteriously raising his hand very high and then lowering it, as if he were conducting some secret symphony. Towards the end you do get a progression of extraordinarily eloquent images of him, each of which comes with, as it were, a just surprise.

It seems to me a model fo the sort of fiction in which you try to meet again and find a better rapport with someone who has been enormously important in your life. Ramsay clearly has that kind of hold or power in Virginia Woolf's imagination and I think her dealing with him is exemplary if you compare it with other novelists who have done anything like it—for instance, it compares very well with D. H. Lawrence's dealing with his father in *Sons and Lovers*.

I put my emphasis on the father because I'm not one of the admirers of Mrs Ramsay. It seems to me she's sufficiently there for the role she has in the novel; but that seems primarily to be kind of luminous *value* by which Ramsay is to be measured and mainly found wanting. I know she is criticised as well as idealised, but it still seems to me that this is mainly what she is. And one gets an odd indication of this in the curious way in which her absence in the third part of the novel seems somehow bigger than her presence in the first part.

* * *

GB: Thank you. . . . I think that one important point that's already been raised is the question of *consensus* of reading. Perhaps that very high place in the canon that *To the Lighthouse* is given is because it is a novel where on the whole people think that there is a consensus of reading. I would like to raise the problem of whether we should, precisely for that reason, look suspiciously at it. But perhaps before we develop that argument, I could turn to Iris Murdoch to hear something of her reaction to Virginia Woolf.

IM: I'm not quite sure how to begin. I don't feel that she comes at all near my own work, though I admire her very much. She is usually associated with the term "stream of consciousness," which we've been thinking about in relation to both the previous talks [Hermione Lee's and Allen McLaurin's], and when I first read her when I was at school I was interested in this conception. But I was chiefly, I think, concerned with her as a *novelist*. I mean, she may have *hoped* that she was going to have—or thought she *might* if she were really free—no humour or characters or plot, but she *did* have these things! And I think one's reflection upon the characters—and we've just heard Mr Harvey talking about this—is one of the main sources of interest in her. The "stream of consciousness" method is in many respects, of course, more familiar to us now as a way of protraying character. The change in people's attitude to her is interesting to a critic, to a historian, also perhaps to a philosopher; we now see a very different, at least I now see a very different Virginia Woolf, from the one we saw earlier.

The matter of her feminism is a rather delicate one, I think, which one has to pick up with a good deal of care. Perhaps we both recognise her feminism now and are critical of it. That is, we see, on the one hand, that she's a fighter for the position of women (and the reference to Jane Harrison I find interesting). On the other hand, there's an awful lot in her stories which is to do with portraying a feminine sensibility in contrast to a masculine intellect, or a feminine generosity in comparison with a male egotism; and I don't think that I see the world in quite those terms. Nor do I think that the liberation of women should be associated with such distinctions.

So I think that she is of continuing interest, to critics of course, and to thinkers generally. And she's a great extraordinary phenomenon really. I mean, the notion of stream of consciousness is now everywhere among us, and is practised in a great many ways, but there's nobody quite like her. And this phenomenon remains with us in the great open free society of the novel, where people do, in spite of critics, do all sorts of different things.

GB: I think the point you made at the end there is certainly one we all ought to bear in mind. . . . An inhibition at the moment with Virginia Woolf is the tendency to see her always in the intellectual group of Bloomsbury. I would rather like to see her alongside some other modernist writers like Henry Green, or even Ivy Compton-Burnet. I wonder what you, Bernard, would think about that kind of grouping?

BB: Yes, well it's very curious the way her reputation was occluded, as I said, for a long time, and then came up again; and one can trace the sort of stages of the ascent. And I think the Bloomsbury cult which perhaps reached its peak a few years ago, that this *was* rather factitious. And yes, I think you're right, this didn't do her any good; to be all the time placing her into that particular historical/social/cultural context. I suppose, yes, as Iris says, the feminism is something which has made her now so much the focus of attention. I recently read, I think it was for the first time, her *A Room of One's Own*, which I suppose is one of the main planks in her use by feminists, which is a very eloquent, polemical book. I really don't know how usable I would find it if I were a late twentieth century woman. I mean, clearly some of the arguments are very inspiring; I think the whole notion of patriarchy seems to have been taken out of that book, the way she uses it. But I would have thought many of her other arguments and assumptions are very much of an earlier milieu and period. But certainly that's another thing which has helped her reputation now.

And then there's the minute latter-day interest, not just in stream of consciousness, but in all modes of narrative. A fairly recent critical discovery has been that you can write *endlessly* about, not a single book, but two or three pages, by the sort of minute analysis of narrative modes; and as sophisticated and subtle a writer as Virginia Woolf offers a great deal of scope here. But that takes it a long way from the kind of interest John Harvey spoke of; a purely *human* interest in how you get your father sorted out or focussed in a work of fiction. That is a solid, traditional interest in characters, psychology and so on—which I think still appeals—but there's a lot of latter-day interest in Virginia Woolf of a rather technical kind that is fascinated by the sheer complexity of her narrative. In short, Virginia Woolf has become a great object of academic *study*. Bearing in mind her dismissive comments about the academic study of English, there's a deep irony about this: what would she have made of all of us, sitting here, in these deliberations? That's a deeper question. I don't know whether anyone would like to sketch in an answer to that. . . .

GB: I'm not really sure I much care what she'd have made of us. It seems to me that a writer writes, the writing becomes usable in a variety of ways, and that those uses are determined by historical moments. She certainly potentiated in her novels elements that she would not necessarily herself have recognised; just as, I think, she potentiated in her novels rereadings of the Victorian writers; she dispersed them into a kind of discourse that they certainly couldn't have recognised or composed for themselves. I think that in the same way there is a dispersal of the parents in *To the Lighthouse*. So when we get to *Between the Acts* and she says "Dispersed are we" (or rather "it is said" and it is said deliberately at several removes in that narrative), the saying is not at all negative. Dispersal may be something that we can draw from Virginia Woolf that she had very little awareness of in her career, but which she needed and which she performed.

In the same way, the question about her adoption by—well you called it, and I think Iris called it, feminism—clearly one would have, if one were going to try to plot her reputation, to distinguish quite acutely between different forms of feminism. For instance, Elaine Showalter takes her strongly to task for the androgynous drive of her theory and her writing and says that we should instead be setting up a complete opposition between male and female, and should be engaging in something more like gynocriticism, something in which we study only women writers. Whereas I think I don't agree with Showalter there, because it seems to me that one of the things that Woolf does, and allows us to do, is to get outside some of these binarisms, such as male-female, so that we don't need to take necessarily a kind of post-

Leech view of myth, as always implying Night and Day. All right, I know she uses all these oscillating contraries in her own work. But it does seem to me that she prepares us also simultaneously to question this particular kind of oscillation of contraries.

Getting away from oppositions which create despondency, that's one of the things that I (reading her as a woman who writes, though who doesn't write novels) find that she allows me to think about, and develop. But I don't claim it as something that only feminist criticism permits, but as available to any of us reading her—in the eighties. We're here, after all, reading her in the eighties, not in the twenties or thirties.

IM: I'm not quite sure what I should be picking up here, but perhaps I could just say a few things that I think. This matter of myth is very much in people's minds now, and I think should be, partly because of our attitude toward religious myth, and the demythologisation of religion, and wondering what myth does for us, and so on. One has to remind oneself with a novelist, that this is a work of art and that the novelist is making up his own myth; and that one has to look at all these things in the context of the whole work. This is important in relation to the imagery that she uses, and the method of her stream of consciousness. I think this is a terribly deep and difficult problem. Hermione Lee very eloquently and movingly presented this image of a perceived thing which becomes the thought and feeling, and how these things are, as it were, glued together—which is in itself, in a way, an image of art. Somebody could say, though perhaps it would be misleading, about Virginia Woolf, that she was always writing about art. That she was thinking about this peculiar transformation.

Now, I think this is a difficult thing to judge. If somebody says to me offhand, well now, what makes you enjoy reading Virginia Woolf? I might say, "She's full of marvellous metaphors; there are the most wonderful images which one wants to remember." And in this respect she is like a poet. But again, it's very important that she's not a poet. . . . One has to try both to enjoy the magic—and she's a great magician—and also to try and assess the truth of what is being said. Is it something deep that's being said? Is it something interesting? Is it something true? And this is where the fact that it is a story is important; it is about characters, and the contrast which John Harvey made between the figure of Mrs Ramsay and the figure of Mr Ramsay brings this out I think. That Mrs Ramsay is a sort of luminous value—one might compare her, *mutatis* a great many *mutandis*, with Cordelia in *King Lear*, who is both a person and a kind of luminous symbol. Well now, some people, and I think I rather half feel this myself, react against

Mrs Ramsay. They think there's a bit too much luminosity based on not enough *stuff*, and that Mr Ramsay is a more interesting and *realistic* (let the word come in here) character.

And one has to think of this tremendous presentation in terms of images, as something which has also to be seen as part of a work of art, written in discursive prose. And that the *transformation*—and this is where the difficult bit comes that I can't really explain—the transformation of the image into a kind of *thing* (this is a way people sometimes talk about some kinds of poetry, perhaps T. S. Eliot does) . . . this is something which can be seen to be valuable for itself. But the *truth* of it, the truth-conveying aspect of it, the reality-conveying aspect of it, or the sense in which it is something which transcends its mere charm, will depend upon its relation to the whole narrative. So the stories are important, and indeed the plot is important. I do think that it is an important objection to some of the novels, or to parts of some of the novels, when various plots are suggested, that the sort of truth-structure within which the stream of consciousness is going to gain its finest quality, is inhibited, is not present, because of the absence of some kind of dominating intellect, which of course Virginia Woolf is deliberately inhibiting.

JH: I think the point which I'd like to make especially is that in *To the Lighthouse* particularly the concern for truth involves the presence of irony. I think, by the way, that Virginia Woolf is always, to an extent, a realist, that she is a realist in the sense that there always seems to be some check and a test on her characters as to whether each next step they take is plausible. I think that applies, for instance, even in *The Waves*, the novel which, in its style of language, can seem furthest away from any realistic mode. Still, the characters of Jinny, Bernard and so on, seem to be checked against an idea Virginia Woolf has as to how each of them would feel in reality, however stylised and poetic their speeches are.

I think this kind of appraisal of the characters in the fiction, against some fairly direct sense of the world as it is, is operating all the time. But I agree with Iris Murdoch that it does often seem to operate weakly, and in *The Waves* I think it operates weakly. I think what enables it to operate more strongly in *To the Lighthouse* is the presence of irony. You get in that novel, I think especially with Mr Ramsay, a variety of response, a variety of ironic inflections. It's noticeable, for instance, that in almost any one of those long sentences which Mr Ramsay inspires, Virginia Woolf will start off with a fairly hostile irony—that at times he'll sound like Mr Gradgrind in Dickens—and yet the sentence will wind its way round and inside Ramsay's ego, and see things somewhat in his perspective also, so that the irony takes a different tinge, more sympathetic, and is at times benign.

Involved with the irony there is also the extraordinary mobility of viewpoint that you get in *To the Lightouse* as Virginia Woolf moves constantly from character to character, and circles and returns, enters one person's passion and another person's fancy, then recedes to a distance and sees things in a long perspective: she's so mobile that the reader is constantly engaged, as she is, in comparing and appraising.

The ironic inflections that keep entering the prose do, I think, work as indirect but constant checks as to truth, and this is why I think that because there is less irony there is less truth in her subsequent fiction (except of course for *Between the Acts* which is ironic everywhere). In this connection I'd like to take up another point that Gillian made, and question the value of dispersal. Dispersal is certainly something that Virginia Woolf is interested in, and one would want to take more of a stand in relation to it than simply to say that it is a good object of study. Because I'd have thought that the strength of *To the Lighthouse* is that she doesn't attempt to disperse the discrepant features of, for instance, Ramsay, but keeps them together; while in, for instance, *Mrs. Dalloway*, she took the decision at a fairly early stage to disperse the conception she had originally had—of a person for whom the social world had very strong holds and in whom the genius of a hostess was strong, but for whom all that social busyness could collapse into solitary and suicidal dejection. That conception which, it seems to me, could have led to a character who would have been both as much in her heart and under her skin as Mr Ramsay, and which could have generated as fine a fiction, was dispersed into Mrs Dalloway on the one hand and Septimus Smith on the other. It seems to me that more is lost than is gained with that dispersal. Again, *The Waves* seems dominated by the idea that the several characters in it are the dispersed parts of a kind of ideal, whole person, whom in a way is figured by the dead Percival, but whom one is also meant to imagine being composed by the remaining lives. And it seems to me here again that the conception doesn't work.

* * *

GB: Could I . . . come back to you, Bernard? Because it seems to me that a real, a quite crucial disagreement is coming out, which is that, if I were asked for the novels which I most value in Virginia Woolf's work, they would be two of those that have so far come in for the greatest demurral, that is *Mrs Dalloway* and *The Waves*, and then I think I'd go on to *Between the Acts*. And that probably is to do with the deep attachment that I have—which

I think is something more than an object of study—to the idea of *dispersal.* Or, if you like, to *permeation*, getting away from the ordering of a plot, which relies on certain authoritarian knittings up, and instead allows things to move out and not necessarily be completed. I wouldn't myself see this as in any way a reneging on plot, but rather as a new form of narrative which queries our implicitly patriarchal concepts of plot. Thus I would be interested to hear what Bernard, for instance, would say if he were composing a canon of Virginia Woolf—which books would go into it as the ones which he would most wish to read again?

BB: Well, I suppose if one is compiling a canon—which I might say I don't find a terribly interesting activity—but if one were to then, yes, it would be *To the Lighthouse* I think. But as people have been talking, as John Harvey was talking about realism and so on, certain thoughts were coming together in my mind—which is that we have come increasingly to fit Virginia Woolf into a sort of modernist pantheon, and to say that she embodies the modernist aesthetic, which is all sort of tied up in a convenient shorthand myth, timelessness, narration dissolved into epiphanies and moments and gestures toward transcendence, the undermining of conventional narrative—all of that. At this point, you know, I start thinking like a Marxist, which I am not, but they are the necessary opponents in my own inner dialogues, . . . I can see ways where she clearly does fit very significantly into twentieth century history: *Mrs. Dalloway*, among other things, is a novel about what happens to English life after the First World War; that War is a visible, rather terrible presence in the book in Septimus Smith, who dies. But when she comes to *To the Lighthouse* she seems to move away from that kind of realism, she seems to move much more to myth, to transcendence, epiphanies and all the rest of it . . . And I'm often fascinated by that momentary appearance the First World War makes in *To the Lighthouse*, in square brackets I think, in that sort of middle section which is a kind of brief summary of what's gone on. One of the young men has died, other young men have too—all of this is just so summarily treated that I'm sometimes rather shocked by this. How *could* she, as it were, dispose of such a historical disaster and catastrophe in such a brief compass. It seems rather a sort of aesthetic indifference.

But thinking about it again, one can see that it's a sufficient clue to something. . . . In other words, one way of looking at *To the Lighthouse* is to relate it to certain other major English novelists of the twenties which have the First World War as a kind of invisible presence. *Women in Love* is one obvious example. As Paul Delaney said in his recent book, it's one of the greatest war novels in which the War is never actually mentioned. Forster's *A Passage to India* is another one, which is set far away in space, and is not very clear about its time, but probably before the War. But the War is clearly permeating the book in terms of the personal disruption that Forster suffered and underwent following it. *To the Lighthouse* is a third of these; it came out in 1927, and the War is all but invisible, but it is nevertheless there, momentarily. I mean it would be a perfectly respectable critical thing to say, "So what?" It's not really like *A Passage to India* or *Women in Love* at all; it's much more personal, aesthetic, symbolic, and that might be a thing to argue about. But that momentary presence does fascinate me.

We then come to her last novel, *Between the Acts*, which, as one bit of homework for this conference, I reread, for the first time in many years, and enjoyed very much. I thought, well this is a book much more *open* to history. I mean it was written after the Second World War had started, and it is placed at that particular moment, very precise in time, June 1939. And though the pageant looks back in various, I think sometimes rather factitious ways at English history, there is also the fact that war is impending, and certain stock properties of the 1930s are actually *there*—like aeroplanes flying over. And I think that book can be related to other books of the late thirties and early forties which to my mind focus that particular moment in history, the period 1938–39: Louis MacNeice's *Autumn Journal*, Orwell's *Coming Up For Air*, and a rather less well known book, very good, Patrick Hamilton's *Hangover Square*, which is set precisely in the period 1938–39, and *ends* on the day when the Second World War broke out. So this is perhaps a rather unusual perspective in which to see Virginia Woolf, but maybe it's a way of taking her, in this particular novel, out of the normal Woolf context, the modernist context, and placing it into a number of books that do illuminate from within a very crucial historical moment.

GB: Yes, I'm actually amazed, if I can jump in before everyone else, . . . to hear you saying that there's just a sort of fleeting reference to the First World War in *To the Lighthouse*, because it seems to me that the whole section "Time Passes" is the period of the War, that there is a very strong sense of cataclysm, of the thing dissolving . . . The book won't hold together, is shattered apart by this central section, and she's making the effort that Lawrence also made in what was to be *The Sisters*—to hold a family history in one place, in one piece. He couldn't do it because of the intervention of the First World War; she just about does it, but she does it by having this extrusion of the War, with references to it which make quite clear what's going on; what's that boat doing? Why is it going down? The whole of that section is *full* of references to the War. Certainly I would agree with you about *Between the Acts*; it's a highly political novel, and one which, I think, is very properly to be connected strongly to *Three Guineas* and her feelings about militarism and to the advent of the Second World War. But in *To the Lighthouse*, I just can't see the War as absent; I've always seen it as absolutely there.

BB: I'm willing to take correction from you there, Gillian, because I did not actually look up the passage; I'm just talking off the top of my head. I thought it was briefer than you tell me it is. But I think it is still true that most people's memories of *To the Lighthouse* are of other things than that middle section.

IM: I think I agree with Gillian here on this point about *To the Lighthouse.* I thought the device of the square brackets in which terrible events were very briefly recorded was successful, had got a kind of tragic point to it, that one felt that this was going on and somehow these brief things conjured it up very well. This makes me want to say something about *The Voyage Out* which nobody seems to want to put on their list, but which I like very much. I think my two favourites would be *To the Lighthouse* and *The Voyage Out.* I like it because perhaps Virginia Woolf was doing something there which she later decided was improper for her to do, and that is to tell a terribly sad story in great detail. I think that the second part of *The Voyage Out* is a very good novel. And it's something which reminds me of Conrad (who I think, incidentally, is a better writer, but that's by the way). It's something which Conrad might have done . . . the notion of the visit to the village, the mysteriousness, the ambiguity, the fear, and then the tragedy ensuing. I think this is marvellous. And there are little touches in *To the Lighthouse* which seem to me to have that sort of tragic force also. . . .

I'm worried about *Mrs. Dalloway* and the business of dispersion and permeation—though you did say that this is in fact a way of doing a plot; the plot doesn't disappear, it is just part of this pattern. I think that one can go too far in the direction of dispersion, through images becoming sort of self-directed pleasures instead of being the servant of some other idea. And the danger of writing this, what one might rather crudely call "poetic prose," is that invention at this level can sometimes inhibit really *deep* invention. I look for really deep inventions in her work, and I think there are a number of them. But I think that sometimes she, as I said before, deliberately decides that she won't make deep inventions.

GB: Now I think we can throw this open to the floor; there were a couple of people with questions . . .

Teresa Vanneck-Murray: I've got about twenty points now, and I'm going to be in a muddle. But I'd like to go right back to the beginning and, with all due respect to Bernard, whom I know, and to John, whom I don't know, say that I don't know why we haven't got four women novelists up there, because I do believe that Virginia Woolf is important as a woman writer and to us now. I don't belong to any particular group of feminist thinking, but I really do think she must be approached as a woman. Now when John was talking, he was talking in a very masculine fashion about things, about *negotiation* especially. And it seems to me that what comes out of that book is how the *woman* negotiates this concern with her father—a father for a woman is a quite different person from a father for a man—and it also tells us something about how women negotiate within their society, within the spectrum of things they have to see to, within their families for instance, a point which also comes out in *Mrs. Dalloway.* It seems to me that in her work we have got the stream of consciousness done in very feminine terms, without being stupidly or sugarily feminine. . . . The whole approach, it seems to me, is as a woman, and this is why I think Virginia Woolf has been neglected. Yet suddenly we see . . . a great mass of women; I've never been to a Conference with so many women in it. And I think that this is because she *does* say something, she does have perceptions about how a lot of women (one can't possibly say all) perceive experience, deal with experience, and about how women negotiate with the society they are a part of—very often as rather invisible presences. We *are* invisible presences, except for here. . . . Now women are coming to the fore Virginia Woolf is becoming more and more appreciated, because she is being appreciated by half the population that were invisible before. . . .

GB: Okay. [applause] Before I hand it back to John and Bernard [laughter] is there someone else? Hermione?

Hermione Lee: Yes, it was just to raise a point in pursuit of what Bernard Bergonzi was saying, which actually is in contradistinction to what's just been said. This is to pursue comparison you mentioned between Virginia Woolf and Henry Green. The question is: why should modernism have to be in another bag from realism? We have been talking about her as a modernist, but it is perhaps more interesting to talk about her in this group of 1930s realist writers, leading up to the War. If you put *Between the Acts* with *Party Going*—which is a book which I thought you might mention but didn't—what you've got are two modernist texts, in that they are highly formalist—*Between the Acts* relying heavily on the process of fragmentation, *Party Going* being an extremely mannered, contained, odd narrative—but both about the imminence of the War as it affects a particular class. They both seem to me to be about something you may call historical, to be historical novels if you like, and also to be modernist texts in the way you've been talking about modernism. As a footnote one might say Henry Green is a male writer, *Virginia Woolf* is a female writer; but I think there is a considerable overlap in what they're doing.

BB: Well I think I would agree with that; I think it's a valuable comparison with *Party Going*. And yes, I suppose there's no real reason why realism and modernism shouldn't go together. I've probably had my mind blown by reading so much criticism which says that no realism is totally finished, that a text is a text is a text, and that word and world have no relation . . . and I'm coming back to find it's not true after all.

JH: I fear I lack the essential qualification to give a proper answer to the questioner before last. I'd have thought, however, that her question would confirm that it is especially male authority, male ego, that gets under women's skin, as it were, and that it does therefore actually seem a fit subject for a novel by a woman. . . . I wouldn't want to try to speak about areas of experience where she may be very good but where I'm in a sense disqualified from speaking. I wonder though, where she is best at that? The novel I've got in my mind as one of the good ones is *Night and Day*, which I reread recently and which seemed to me very direct and sensitive and strong in its approach to just those questions about feminine experience which you were raising. . . . I really am not clear and would be glad for guidance as to indications of strength in the representation of distinctively feminine experience in the later fiction.

GB: Would you like to come back on that? Or is there another woman who would like to speak to this?

Sandra Lummis: It seems to me interesting that in the two earlier novels Virginia Woolf does particularly talk about women being attracted to men because they see the *woman* in the man; that she refers to them as in fact having feminine sensibilities. Indeed, Rachel and Katherine eventually accept their suitors for this reason. I don't think this comes up particularly in the later novels, but certainly in those two early ones this is very much felt.

Leena Kore: I think it is not so much that one shouldn't be sympathetic to the fact that a woman can respond to a fiction in the way she described herself responding. But the difficulty I have is that Virginia Woolf herself is constantly aiming towards an androgyny. She herself would say that all the greatest novelists were sexless—I think that's a direct quotation. And it's a difficulty that I would have because I think that, ultimately, she would be very unhappy if we remained on the sides of either men or women as regards her fiction. I don't know how you would answer that, but I think it is a problem.

Margaret Bonfiglioli: I'd like to make some links between some of the things which have come up; and to do so, I have to make use of the word "*reality*," which has a very peculiar relation to the word "realism" in the way in which Virginia Woolf uses it. And she uses it—I'm afraid I can't tell you exactly where—to talk about the "reality" behind appearances. I think that in her novels one gets a sort of *surface* realism, but that beneath that she's going for some kind of truth which perfectly ordinary people seem to perceive through mystical experiences. But mystical experiences are not, in our present culture, very easily spoken about—the sort of oceanic feelings of oneness and so on, which, say, the Oxford Religious Experience Unit is able to collect in a way that suggests that forty per cent of the population have them, and that the nonliterary, or not specially literary population, have them. Some of the people who have those experiences think that they're mad, because there isn't a way, or because they're out of touch with the traditional ways of talking about them. Now, it seems to me that some of what we might call feminine experience in Virginia Woolf isn't really confined to women at all, but comes into this area of rather "unspeakable" experience which our present culture isn't very sympathetic to. . . . I'd like to make some connections with the pursuit of truth in Virginia Woolf and the idea of some kind of "reality," which is I suppose what some people mean by transcendence.

GB: Thank you. . . . Iris, would you like to come back into this discussion?

IM: Well I felt a lot of sympathy with the last speaker. I would see the best of what she does in this kind, the searching for "reality" behind appearances, which I think describes what all good artists are trying to do. This takes a particular form with her because of the tremendous net of glittering appearances which she spreads out. I would sympathise with your picturing this as a kind of *ordinary* mysticism—not any sort of weird mysticism, but the intensity of present experience thought of as part of the *value* of the person's mode of being, the value of their consciousness. And this question of value coming in is, I think, important and deep, and is to do with truth. I mean is truth here being displayed? I would certainly connect that with a notion of mysticism and truth, and the word "transcendence" being in place—though all this would have to be explained rather carefully—rather than mixing it in any way *in* with feminine sensibility.

Ian Gregor: I wonder if I could just come back to a point Hermione was making about wanting to get away from notions of modernism and realism being separate. I can see why you would want to do that, but at the same time it does seem to me that to consider Virginia Woolf as a modernist is very helpful in the sense that it seems to me her art is very much an art of allusion and of hint, and that there is behind the novels an unwritten story which is, I think, very much a point about the novelist's art. We've talked about Henry Green, but I think there's a very fruitful comparison with the archetypal figure of modernism, Eliot himself. The comparisons between "The Waste Land" and *Mrs. Dalloway* are extremely interesting; they both seem to me to get their interest through this art of implication and allusion, and the sense of an unwritten story, rather than through any kind of accumulated story, the detailed story which we associate with realism.

Eric Warner: Could I just pick up on that and see if I can piece together a few things in the discussion? Bernard Bergonzi was talking about the a-historical quality in Woolf, her peculiar relation, at any rate, to what we know as history, and I found myself wondering if this isn't because her sense of history is so dominantly *literary*. She is one of the most well read of a well-read generation, after all, and the sense of allusion that Ian Gregor pointed to, which certainly is there, is almost entirely one of literary allusion. *Between the Acts* is surely the novel where one sees that, inasmuch as the images of past history, in the pageant and so on, are all of literary history. Now I wonder if this doesn't connect with what Iris Murdoch said, that in some ways she was always writing about *art*, which in turn would strengthen the link with Eliot just mentioned, in view of his conception of tradition, where all art is linked to, or has a sense of communion with, other art which has gone before, and all artists, regardless of their particular time, are in this sense reaching toward the same thing. I wonder if you would care to comment on that?

BB: Well, she certainly is a very literary writer, yes indeed; and to some extent sheltered from the most disagreeable historical realities of her time. But only to some extent. She did live through the First World War and its aftermath, and also through a bit of the Second World War. I think, to go back to *Between the Acts*, I mean, yes, of course, it is an extraordinary kind of *literary* work, with its particular kind of English literary-historical consciousness working through the pageant, and all the pastiche and imitation of earlier literary styles. To look at it one way, yes it is overburdened with literary material. And yet, the history is there, the aeroplanes fly over and drown out the sound of the pageant for a while. That, to me, is emblematic of the way in which the harsher aspects of history come in and almost obliterate the sound of literature.

GB: Yes. One of my pupils once pointed out to me that they're collecting money to put new lighting into the church and, of course, the blackout is just about to descend.

Juliet Dusinberre: I think the lady who spoke about feminine experience and about whether there should have been female novelists on the panel, deserves a follow-up. I didn't agree with Dr Harvey about Mrs Ramsay, because as a woman reader I feel Mrs Ramsay is a wonderful portrait of the mothering consciousness, and that the description of her relation with her children is unmatched in literature. The only thing I've read which can compare with it is Tolstoy's portrait of Dolly Oblonsky in *Anna Karenina.* Now when one has said that, one is back at the question of whether one can separate male and female writers, because Tolstoy has evoked marvellously the feelings of a woman about her children, as indeed Virginia Woolf has, even though she herself had no children. I think that while recognising that area as feminine experience one should allow the creative artist, male or female, to explore it.

What is powerful in *To the Lighthouse* is the search of both sexes for permanence. You get this with Mr Ramsay and his books—will they last? And then he goes and reads Scott and thinks: "If this is lasting, my books will last," for, as he says, it is so alive, so full of vigour. In a sense this is what Mrs Ramsay is doing when she says: "You *must* marry; Lily, you must marry, Minta, you must marry," because the way you pass on life and permanence is through having children. What unites both sexes is the concern for how to place permanence against the daily evidence which one sees in the book—and particularly in that war passage—of transcience in human life. I am anxious for this distinguished panel of creative writers to talk about their own work and about whether they are conscious of a search for permanence, or whether they think this is something specific to Virginia Woolf and writers of that time.

IM: To comment first of all on what you said at the beginning, I don't like the idea of feminine experience . . . I think there's human experience; and I don't think a woman's mind differs essentially from a man's, except in the sense that women are often less well educated. The women in Virginia Woolf's stories are always emphasising this fact, that they don't know Latin and Greek and the men do. Well, these things change; now nobody knows Latin and Greek [laughter]. . . . But I think that there are very relevant changes in society, relevant to this discussion, since her time and certainly since Tolstoy's time. You very charmingly tell us about Mrs Ramsay as the ideal mother, then you mention Tolstoy who also does it, so one sees it can be done by either. I think, though, that perhaps for very simple reasons it hasn't been done well in the past, because men and women didn't know each other with such freedom as they do now. I mean, women didn't know men, as is often pointed out about various women writers in the past who found it difficult to portray men, and men didn't really know women. Conrad, for example, had difficulty in portraying women, which is one of the blemishes, I think, in his work. But that's all a sort of footnote to my saying that I don't think there's a female intellect as opposed to a male intellect, or a female artistry, though there are obviously all sorts of accidental features about people's lives which enable them to portray one thing better than another.

But to come to this other thing about transcience and permanence . . . yes, I think that is a deep thing. I certainly feel it in my own work; but there are so many different ways of being concerned with it. I feel concerned with it in relation to the idea of morality. I think it's often a good thing to ask about a philosopher, and maybe about a novelist, what are they afraid of? That's certainly illuminating about philosophers. . . . I think I'm afraid of relativism. I'm afraid of it turning out that it doesn't matter very much how you behave after all, instead of the importance and reality of goodness being something absolute. And I think that great art does convey this; and that Virginia Woolf's novels very often, though not always, can convey it. And in her case, as you say, very beautifully in *To the Lighthouse*, which is concerned with marriage and with permanence under this image.

* * *

JH: It's not clear to me that Mrs Ramsay *is* an ideal mother. That is to say, it's not clear to me that the kind of concern she has for her children and for other people too is offered by the novel as an ideal concern. I would have thought that the novel takes pains to show that a lot of the things she tries to force on people are mistakes, that the marriage she is shown forcing is a mistake, that her prescriptions for Lily Briscoe aren't a help. Actually, I'd have thought that feminine experience and its intensities and difficulties are much more interestingly registered in Lily Briscoe, than they are in Mrs Ramsay. I think Virginia Woolf is most telling on these questions, not in the direct writing about what you feel for your children, but in those *contretemps* where Ramsay comes claustrophobically close to Lily, pressing on her all the exorbitant emotional demands which he feels entitled to make because she's a woman, and which it's clear that he would never make of a man.

Lily also registers very fully and very subtly the problems for any woman wanting to be an artist—and for that matter, a writer—when she ponders the statement "Women can't write, women can't paint." Moreover, she also, just by the way, takes in the question of realism or modernism. It's not clear how abstract Lily's painting is; it clearly has a real subject in the house in front of which she positions her canvas. And yet the way the painting is discussed makes it sound to quite an extent an abstract or modernist work, when she discusses the balancing of what are, for her, masses or squares or large areas of colour in the painting. These are discussed in an abstract manner, but at the same time they are felt by her and by Virginia Woolf to involve balancing emotional claims and realities and truths. Finally, I think that here the novel really does converge on the suggestion of androgyny mentioned before. I'd have thought that is one of the significances of that single line which, for Lily Briscoe, is the completion of her painting and the epitome of her vision, balancing the truths of Mr and Mrs Ramsay. All in all, therefore, I think that she, Lily, is *the* sensitive and interesting feminine focus in the novel.

* * *

GB: Perhaps we could, because there was applause when Juliet Dusinberre suggested we should hear more about people's own novels, and the idea of permanence and aim towards transcendence, perhaps we could now ask Bernard and John if they would like to comment along these lines on their own work.

BB: I don't want to talk about the one brief novel I've published in the same context as a great novelist like Virginia Woolf; I find it rather embarrassing. In Virginia Woolf clearly I think one has got what I take it a lot of major art does, which is to try to save something from the flux. This is perhaps *the* great thing about literature; life is flux and falling away, and one is trying to make something of it, something that will endure, something that will last. And analogies with marriage, childhood and so on are very common—Shakespeare's Sonnets and other Elizabethan literature, and in many other genres. So if she's doing that, and I think she is in *To the Lighthouse*, yes, "create" is the word, surely, create form against dissolution, flux and so on, which by analogy is perhaps what human life is all about. I mean I think one is getting rather exalted, into rather vague terms perhaps; but I think we all understand the underlying gesture. I would certainly accept Juliet's analysis and leave it at that.

JH: Likewise I don't feel it's appropriate to start talking about myself here. Virginia Woolf is clearly concerned with permanence, especially with finding right moments which epitomise someone, the moments by which they are to be associated, to be remembered, which represent them at their best. I'd have thought, to refer tiresomely to Mr Ramsay again, that for him it would be that moment where he leaves the boat and jumps onto the rock, as if he were saying (as perhaps he had as a young man) "There is no God," but also with his youth seen in his movements. This is the moment which the novel opts for as its last glimpse of him; this, if anything is to preserve him for permanence. She seems to have an interest in this sort of moment and the kind of timelessness it might have.

GB: And that is a moment of high comedy as well as deep feeling, it seems to me. I was very struck when right at the beginning Iris Murdoch was commenting on the comedy and the characters and the plot. . . .

One of the most curious things about Virginia Woolf's work is that she is a superb comic writer, but that we tend, somehow, not to talk about that. I think it is partly because on the page the abrasions and difficulties (the ways in which the shifting scale of comedy function) are smoothed out by the silence of narrative. If any of her work is read aloud, people start to laugh. But what *voice* is that aloud voice that is reading it? Is there a real obliteration of voice in her text?

In order for the comedy not to become supreme, is there a kind of silence in her narrative? Or should we sometimes read her aloud, restore the voice? Hear it as a woman's voice speaking, making comic difficulties in the text? But perhaps, Iris, I could turn to you and ask you if you could say a bit more about the idea of comedy in her work.

IM: Well, I think that humour and comedy are very important in the novel, and it's difficult to think of any great novel which lacks these, whether in the form of irony, or in the form of what one might call the deep comic, the sort of Shakespearian comic, which is a great and marvellous form and very much at home in the novel. I would personally restrict the word "tragedy." There are no tragedies in life; tragedy is an idea that belongs to art, and to very few bits of art; there are very few tragedies really. Comedy is everywhere in human life, and is also everywhere in art, and of course particularly in the novel. I was thinking again about Mrs Ramsay, how characters are *saved* by the funny bits, which, as Gillian was saying, we sometimes tend to forget because of some dominating feeling we have about a writer. For instance, Dostoevsky is an *extremely* funny writer, but people think of him always as a terribly intense, quasi-religious, dramatic writer. And thinking of Mrs Ramsay, I like the bit where the Mannings are mentioned and someone remarks that they've got a billiard room now, which surprises her; "the *Mannings* have got a *billiard* room!" And then she thinks, "But I haven't thought about them for years," and then she thinks "Perhaps they haven't thought about me for years either" . . . [laughter]

Ellman Crasnow: Yes, we might take this idea of comedy a little further, extending it beyond character by going back to what's been said about women's writing. I think most of the interventions from a feminist point of view have been on the lines of feminine critiques of gender behaviour, models of male and female, etc. But there is also a feminist critique that applies to the way in which you can or cannot speak, because certain institutions give you a discourse. Now there's no doubt that Woolf was very aware of this—there's ample evidence to that effect—so that she simply has an adversary relationship to most of her received models of narrative discourse. And among other things, this seems to make for a great deal of comedy: when I think of, say, the ironic narrator of *Orlando*, this is one of the things that always makes me laugh.

Deferred Action in *To the Lighthouse*

Perry Meisel

With Virginia Woolf, we move to the middle ground—the switch or circuit—between Forster's taxonomic reflexive realism and Strachey's historiographical one. Before proceeding to our focus on Woolf's consummate achievement, *To the Lighthouse* (1927)—her *Lear* to the *Hamlet* of *Mrs. Dalloway* (1925), to which we shall briefly turn first—it is worth noting that Woolf is not only a literary corridor between Forster and Strachey, but also an exemplary—and reflexive—participant in Bloomsbury's collective sensibility by virtue of her outrageous borrowings (especially from *Howards End*) of phrases that become perhaps more familiar as tropes in her own prose ("rainbow bridge," "prose and passion"); even of organizing conceits such as Pointz Hall's doubling of Howards End in *Between the Acts* (1941). To call it borrowing or theft, however, is to maintain a sense of private property, literary or otherwise, that Bloomsbury itself must reject because it knows the notion is little more than an illusion and proper authority little more than a transpersonal function.

To speak of *Mrs. Dalloway* as we might wish—as the perfect whole it seems to be—is, of course, as critically problematic as it is to speak seriously of anything categorically autonomous. Like Pater and Forster, Woolf, too, submits the Arnoldean ideal of the proper to interrogation, clearest perhaps in the passage cited earlier from *Between the Acts*, in which the instance of music serves her, as it does Pater, as an especially clear example of the difference underlying all signification, and of the temporal or belated structure of its action. Like *Howards End*, *Mrs. Dalloway* is not an expression of the

From *The Myth of the Modern: A Study in British Literature and Criticism after 1850.* Yale University Press, 1987.

will to modernity, but a catalogue of the kinds of modernist ideals temporality or belatedness disallows, together with an enormously lucid account of the larger structure of modernism that produces such ideals symptomatically. The novel's own appearance of unity is therefore aligned with the customary ideal unities it presents in a number of registers (the pastoral nostalgia of Bourton, for example), chief among them the self. In perhaps the novel's most famous scene, Clarissa, (re)composing her selfhood before her mirror, thinks of herself as a "diamond." And yet—in a strategy like Forster's—the trope's identification elsewhere in the novel with precisely that public world to which it is opposed contaminates the privacy it otherwise signifies here. After all, "diamond" resonates with the novel's seemingly unrelated tropology of finance, empire, and the material resources of colonialism "where only spice winds blow," a tropology into whose range "diamond" may vibrate so as to make it signify a specific type of imperial wealth, and that suggests Clarissa's personal wholeness to be dependent in turn upon the stability of her husband's money. The identification of psychic and real economy is as exact as Forster's: the language of privacy and that of common or public mythologies are once again the same. Woolf's like figuration of Clarissa as now "disinterested" in Sally Seton resonates with the figure of Richard's apparently contrasting "deposit" of affection for her, both terms conjoining in the tropology of imperial riches, and setting off a series of familiar Bloomsbury puns such as Clarissa's desire to "repay" or "pay back" sentiments, the crowd's "unspent" emotions early in the novel, even the ironic "treasures" of Septimus's psychosis. "Signs," in short, "were interchanged." *Mrs. Dalloway* is little less than a textbook of the "shuffle" of "sunken meanings" in words, as Woolf herself presents it in "Craftsmanship," a strategic discourse of puns disguised (like Forster's, but unlike Joyce's overt ones) within the apparent semantic stability of common idioms.

Woolf's ambivalence about belief in the fiction of property, or, as she calls it in *Mrs. Dalloway*, "Proportion"—Farfrae's machine now in the unabashedly antiseptic garb of the doctors Holmes and Bradshaw—is evident in Clarissa's own ambivalence about her social standing and consequent double values ("bring part of it" on the one hand, being "outside, looking on" on the other). It is even more evident in Woolf's (later) construction during the draftings of the novel of a "double" (1928) for Clarissa who flaunts Proportion with as much calculation as she cultivates it. Septimus, after all, is Clarissa's exact opposite, not shackled by the epistemological impossibility of pure selfhood or "properness," since he gives in entirely to the public determinations that undermine any pure privacy in any case, allowing all Proportion to fall away. Clarissa instead represents just that citizenly contrast that produces ego over against the schizophrenia as displayed by Septimus himself.

Hence both the advertising airplane and the motor-car early in the novel demonstrate not only the determinate reality of public languages in the world itself—now overtly a product of a political or ideological unconscious, a set of shared cultural presuppositions or representations—but also the ways in which such public symbols or languages send given spectators into distinct worlds of private thought. Like the various clocks which strike a few moments apart in relation to the central authority represented by Big Ben, the particularities that fashion privacy are each permutational instances of the dominant ideological arrangements of culture at large.

If *Mrs. Dalloway* recapitulates Forster's strategy of identifying private and public through the language of a text that reflexively enacts their interdependence at the level of the representations that form the world as such, *To the Lighthouse* goes on to identify the mechanism of belatedness with the mechanism of the text's own readability. As elegant an elegy as there is in English (its dialogical relations to *Lycidas*, *Adonais*, and *In Memoriam* are especially exorbitant), *To the Lighthouse* is Woolf's greatest novel if not her best one. The problems the novel sets out to address—the now-twinned thematic and dynamic of temporality or belatedness—are in fact just the kind that make a wholly perfect novel impossible. We have already seen rather briefly why such exact proportion is impossible in the apparently perfect *Mrs. Dalloway*; *To the Lighthouse*, published only two years later, takes the process logically further—to the summit, in fact, of Woolf's career as a novelist. Thus the reader of *To the Lighthouse* must technically experience the very kind of deferred action with which the book is thematically concerned, a consummate example of reflexive realism in which Woolf makes *récit* and *histoire* versions one of the other even as their differences are manifestly preserved. Linear though it may seem, the novel is done in what Pound would call "medallion" style, so that its three component parts may be shifted and rearranged in their relations to one another. Thus entirely different meanings may be inflected by the same parts depending upon the different relations among them one chooses to inflect. Do we read the novel as Mr. Ramsay reads—linearly, in the strictly chronological unfolding that characterizes his reading of Scott's *Antiquary* (as well as the alphabetical order by which he figures his career)? Or do we read in the manner of Carmichael's "acrostics," not unlike Mrs. Ramsay's equally contrasting way of reading "at random," "backwards, upwards" instead? Which part of the novel, in other words, is early and which late? By the temporal schema of years, of course, part 1 obviously precedes part 3 by ten years; by the temporal schema of hours, however, part 3 precedes part 1, since it begins in the morning and concludes at noon, while part 1 begins in the afternoon and ends in the evening.

If we follow the linear trajectory of years, consonant with Mr. Ramsay's linear mode of reading books, we follow the narrative as seems only natural, with part 1 coming first. By so taking part 1 as the origin it seems to be, however, the novel predictably enacts a myth of the modern—the fall from the plenitude of Mrs. Ramsay's Edenic presence that renders the later part 3 a fall into time and history. From this point of view, the priority of fathers oppresses sons and daughters alike; the sundering of " 'subject' " and " 'object' " leaves the question of " 'the nature of reality' " in doubt; and the status of art remains one of recapturing secondarily some primariness forever behind it as both inspiration and inhibition. With the fiction of linear or chronological priority thus positing a myth of origins in Mrs. Ramsay from which all else is a fall or loss, we move, then, from a state of paradisiacal grace in part 1 (despite the twilight mood of its broody pastoral and the northerliness of its site in the Hebrides) to a state of wishful modernist redemption and resurrection in part 3—Oedpial (James and Cam); philosophical (Mr. Ramsay); and aesthetic (Lily).

If, on the other hand, we follow both the diurnal schema as well as the models of reading offered by Carmichael and Mrs. Ramsay, part 3 may be put first instead. Part 1 remains, to be sure, a myth of origins, but now a self-conscious myth retroactively (re)produced by memory. This second reading or arrangement of the novel's parts gives us not only a nonlinear trajectory, but a trajectory rather exactly in accord with the structure of deferred action or belatedness that cautions the myth of the modern and even accounts for the sequence of normative modernist primacies it engenders by presenting James's Oedipus, Mr. Ramsay's philosophical quiddity, and the autonomy of Lily's art. Such a rearrangement tells us, not that we have experienced an irreparable dissociation from Mrs. Ramsay's luminous sensibility, but rather that that which comes early is really a function of that which succeeds it. Belatedness is specified as the poetry of bereavement, as mourning, not just as its token but as its very type, and, in fact, as its very dynamic. Its paradigm is the narrative of memory, in which, as in all narrative, lost presence is produced as a deferred effect of its absence. Thus the novel's production of its world is the result of the remembrance or mourning that necessarily succeeds it, placing reader and narrator alike in an overlapping matrix of desire in which, biographically speaking, the most private of Woolf's writerly compulsions (must one allude to those famous *Diary* entries in which she confesses the book to be a form of mourning for her parents?) becomes a public mode of discourse instead—an elegy.

From this second point of view, then, the novel is no longer another myth of the modern, but an attempt to explain the emergence of such a myth by anatomizing its components, as does Forster, and by subsequently showing how a different shuffling of them may account for the myth they produce. By so reassessing the novel, it becomes a metacritical inquiry into the structure of the modernism that prompts its symptomatic will to modernity as it is concretized in almost everyone's attitude of desire toward Mrs. Ramsay herself.

To begin our reading with the otherwise neglected part 2, then, is logical once we notice that "Time Passes" is at one and the same time the section in which Mrs. Ramsay dies and the one in which the narrator gives us the reflexive counterpart to her loss in the text's language. Much, after all, as Mrs. Ramsay's death flaws the subsequent lives of her family and friends, so the stylistic grumpiness and "reminiscent" landscape of part 2 flaws the novel itself as a literary instance of the belatedness that assails its remaining characters at the level of *histoire* in part 3. Woolf willingly ruins her book in order to give us the ruined landscape of the late Romantic's tropological or imaginative (not mimetic) wasteland in part 2, only, of course, to go on to invent a way of overcoming the loss it represents in the structure of the novel as a whole. The weakest sequence of the book, part 2's awkwardness is about literary weakness itself as the literary-historical precondition under which Woolf must work, and which *To the Lighthouse* as "a whole structure of imagination" will try to outwit and overcome. Unlike Hardy or Forster, however, Woolf does not oppose country and city in order to obtain an image of urban decay and a contrasting one of natural purity. Woolf's rural landscape in part 2 is no more a genuine pastoral retreat than any other such sequences in her fiction (Santa Marina in *The Voyage Out*, the frosty country interlude in *Night and Day*, the seaside in *Jacob's Room*, Bourton in *Mrs. Dalloway*, Pointz Hall in *Between the Acts*). Part 2 is instead (and like these other instances) actually a catalogue of the Romantic tropology of imaginative ruin and despair that is the precondition of belated or modern writing. As Maria DiBattista puts it, part 2 is "a Coleridgean nightmare" (1980). Recalling the common features of Romantic landscape from Blake to Shelley—autumnal and twilight settings, ravaged natural scenes—Woolf's scholarship in "Time Passes" recapitulates the dark and destruction of, for example, the initial movement of *Alastor* or, even more specifically, the imagery of *Adonais*; Coleridge's anxiety in the vale of Chamonix; even the failure of dawn at Snowdon in *The Prelude*. The figure of the "empty" house, too, once filled with life but now marked by Mrs. Ramsay's conspicuous absence, is in turn filiated to a tropological tradition from Bunyan and Keats to Emerson, Pater, and Stevens, in which the "House Beautiful" or "mansion" of literary imagination has become blasted thanks to the increasing burden of precedent by which the history of past usage has incrementally drained from it the possibility of newness or regeneration. Lily Briscoe's name alone should already alert us to the funereal status of all that is supposedly fresh and primary in the novel's northerly setting and September climate. For "Lily," after all, is the flower that signifies death, its customary symbolization already an instance of the reflexive rather than referential status of nature in a novel that, like *Howards End*, is really an account of the status of its representations rather than an expression by or of them.

If part 2 is a catalogue of the past literary usages that make belatedness the precondition of modern literary production, the movement to the lighthouse itself, deferred in part 1 but fulfilled in part 3, is in turn the novel's summary figure for the extent to which it takes the notions of quest-closure and successful allegorization as objects of representation rather than as among its own goals. What are these exemplary quests of which the passage to the lighthouse—to the figure of the Romantic tower—is merely the generic structuring device in this metacritical fiction? Woolf is precise about them: (1) Mr. Ramsay's essentialist philosophical quest for Arnoldean "essences"; (2) James's and Cam's Oedipal drama; and (3) Lily's aesthetic quest. They are a trio of isomorphic allegories not unlike the catalogue of homologous ideals in *Howards End*, and their paradigmatic and distanced structuration in so exact a series of articulations shows them to be three tokens of modernist wish-fulfillment, none sufficiently ironic to account for their merely symptomatic status as impossible desires of the Arnoldean or Eliotic type. The novel puts all three quests in question by adducing them as ideological formations of thought, each contained by the novel rather than recontaining it.

Chief among these overt symbolic quests is Mr. Ramsay's linguistically figured quest for knowledge, the famous attempt to reach beyond the letter Q, to reach the letter of one's own name, an ideal fusion, apparently, of knowledge as such and self-knowledge. Complicit with Mr. Ramsay's linear quest for philosophical knowledge is, of course, Woolf's plain adumbration of its terms, roundly considered ironic today, but historically as well as epistemologically faithful to the issues at hand. As a professional philosopher Mr. Ramsay is certain about his principal topics of contemplation. Though " 'subject and object and the nature of reality' "—Mr. Ramsay's concerns as his children see them—are joked about, these questions are not only to the point, but also have a double historical truth to them. Mr. Ramsay is, after all, continually described in the ebb tide images characteristic of the late Arnold, especially the Arnold of "Dover Beach" or "Calais Sands." Moreover, both his name and that of his protégé, Tansley are the names of two Cambridge academics—Frank Ramsey the philosopher and Arthur Tansley the botanist—with closer personal ties to Bloomsbury than most during the time of the book's composition (Ramsey died in 1926). Mr. Ramsay believes, of course, in "the thing itself", and in the validity of questing for it in the usual positivist way. Like Leslie Stephen's empiricism, Mr. Ramsay's is a prime example of the Cambridge belief in fact—a fact that Woolf, in her enduring antipathy to Moore and his intellectual disciples (Poole 1978), is almost always at pains to include among her objects of scrutiny as surely (as we shall see) as she includes James and Alix Strachey's Freud.

The professional quest of philosophy in part 1, then, becomes Mr. Ramsay's mournful journey to the lighthouse in part 3, now a physical quest for the (ironically symbolic) reality of the thing itself supposedly embodied by the figure of the lighthouse. Woolf allows him his success in part 3, the description even tainted with Christian overtones that, as in Forster, are coterminous with the empiricist philosopher's search for primacy: "He sprang, lightly like a young man, holding his parcel, on to the rock." The lighthouse is indeed as present as a "rock," although such epistemological surety can do nothing to bring Mrs. Ramsay back from the dead. Like the irony of Oedipus, the thing itself turns out to be what it is because it is no more than a symbol for something else, in this case for the type of truth for which its evidence is a mere token even when successful.

If Mr. Ramsay's Arnoldean quest for knowledge is given such exemplary status, so, too, is the overtly Freudian allegory surrounding Mr. Ramsay's son James and, somewhat less so, his daughter Cam. The self-consciousness of Woolf's use of a knowledge of the Oedipus complex—a patent case, though with a difference, of what she herself called, with some contempt, "Freudian Fiction" only seven years before (1920)—is so overt and clinically precise that we ought to be at least as suspicious of it as we traditionally are of Mr. Ramsay's own quest. Our very first look at James in part 1, one recalls all too easily, shows him in the almost ludicrously Oedipal posture of brandishing, in his fancy, a poker with which he will kill the father before the father, at least in his fears, kills him. And much as Mr. Ramsay carries the name of a real contemporary philosopher, so, too, does the name James suggest that of Lytton Strachey's brother, James, translating Freud as Woolf wrote her novels. Part 3 resolves James's Oedipus complex so tidily as to suggest again its status as an ideological bundle rather than as a meaning, much as Mr. Ramsay's success is, at best, real because it is symbolic. The latter may also be symbolic because it is real, but, like the peculiar ironies of the Oedipus complex as *Howards End* details them, the mobility at work in the rhetoric of the establishment of the authority of either an unmediated real or authority itself belies the primacy their like idealities mean to have.

Accompanying both the epistemological and psychoanalytic quests, of course, is Lily's vaunted aesthetic quest, her attempt to conceive and execute her picture. Apparently the double or proving-ground of Woolf's own art,

Lily's aesthetics are, however, like Mr. Ramsay's quest or James's, no more than the third and summary instance of a modernist with subject to critique and correction (even recent attempts to adjust the picture fall short of taking Lily ironically; see Matro, 1984). The nature of Lily's desire for Mrs. Ramsay's love in life in part 1 and for her memory, sanctified by art, after her death in part 3 is the same kind of modernist desire Woolf satirizes in philosophy and psychoanalysis. For Lily in part 1, it is nothing less than a question of discovering the "secret" of Mrs. Ramsay's being (as though, like the unconscious, it were already there):

> She imagined how in the chambers of the mind and heart of the woman who was, physically, touching her, were stood, like the treasures in the tombs of kings, tablets bearing sacred inscriptions, which if one could spell them out, would teach one everything, but they would never be offered openly, never made public. What art was there, known to love or cunning, by which one pressed through into those secret chambers?

There is, implies Woolf, no such "art," and no such "secret chambers" into which it might penetrate. The figuration is ironic enough anyway. Like Trilling's characterization of the desire for a realm beyond culture to be a function of culture's own knowledge, here Lily uses a textual metaphor to represent what she proposes to be instinctual—beyond language or text—in Mrs. Ramsay herself. For Lily in part 3, it is the same question, punctuated now by Mrs. Ramsay's actual loss: "What does it mean, then, what can it all mean?" And despite the clarity with which the commemorative impetus for her painting suggests art to be recursive rather than direct or transcriptive, Lily's aesthetic ideals remain modernist, presuming, like Mr. Ramsay, that an essence or a primacy—an immediacy—lies behind it all: "But what she wished to get hold of was that very jar on the nerves, the thing itself before it has been made anything." The next figure, however, frowns at the will to modernity just expressed: "Get that and start afresh," thinks Lily, "get that and start afresh." Like Arnold's "again begin," the place of origin or singleness is itself one of repetition, already bifurcated as a function of its attempted apprehension. Lily also compounds the problem by recalling Mr. Ramsay's like empiricism in her belief that, "If only she could put [her impressions] together, she felt, write them out in some sentence, then she would have got at the truth of things."

Taken together, this isomorphic trio of ideological or interpretative allegories—each as much a subject of the book as any of its characters—produces an overwhelmingly exact and dramatic closure that the mobile or dynamic structure of the novel at large disallows. Each of the three reaches a dialectical resolution within its own sphere (Mr. Ramsay's combination of success and resignation; James's parturition; Lily's completion of her picture) that together may be said to constitute sufficient unity through homologue for the novel as a whole. The recurrent form of the triangle, moreover, especially visible in the final shape of Lily's painting, stands in turn as a kind of diagram for the resolution or closure each of the dramas seems to produce, but which the novel epistemologically forbids in its simultaneous rejection of all three manifestly successful quests for quiddity, priority, immediacy. Such modernist resolutions are, in short, objects of interpretative reduction, subject as all notions of primacy are to the novel's structural dynamic of deferred action by means of which its own significant form is determined.

It is probably easiest of all to assume that Mrs. Ramsay's power or authority is a function of her enigmatic freshness both in life and in the tenacity with which she remains with her family and friends later on in death. But to trope Mrs. Ramsay as such a lost primacy is, especially given the book's enormous range of epistemological cautions, simply to sanctify another, if grander, myth of the modern to account for a novel whose aim is to thwart all such notions. As the history of Woolf's reception has long demonstrated, it is especially (and dangerously) comfortable to assume that Mrs. Ramsay's heroism is the result of her supposedly exemplary feminity, particularly her elevation to the role of urbane earth mother. And yet femininity, like authority (or, indeed, like any notion in the novel), is necessarily the result of a relation rather than the expression of an essence—masculinity or femininity, or empiricism art, it does not matter. Much as public and private are reciprocal in *Howards End* or *Mrs. Dalloway*, so Mrs. Ramsay's public authority in *To the Lighthouse* is a function of a privacy so profound as finally to have no ego at all by which to name it. Like the paradox of Romantic revelation represented by Septimus, Mrs. Ramsay's most solitary moments are precisely those when she descends so far within as to become part of a without—a world without a self that is, as the self well knows, one of its greatest achievements.

Likewise, Mrs. Ramsay's nurturing femininity is in turn very often an effect of plainly masculine figurations instead. Here especially Woolf gets to impugn the primacy in question—an innate femininity—with decided linguistic zest. Few readers tend to forget the technically masculine potency that has passed over to Mrs. Ramsay's double-duty fertility give the "arid scimitar" of the powerless male. Mrs. Ramsay has ejaculatory qualities as well, as though to confirm Woolf's strategic contamination of metaphorical attributions: "Standing between her knees, very stiff," for example, "James felt all her strength flaring up to be drunk." Hence, too, Lily's characterization of Mrs. Ramsay that we remarked upon earlier is, when revisited, polluted by masculinist metaphors that are obviously, and humorously, out of apparent place. Lily imagines "the chambers of the mind and heart" of Mrs. Ramsay as "like the treasures in the tombs," not of queens, but "of kings." Even her desire to "press . . . through into those secret chambers" is an implicitly phallic figuration, though in the process the now-kingly Mrs. Ramsay is also implicitly switched back into a feminine posture insofar as the "secret chambers" must, in the unavoidably phallic role they assign to Lily, restore to Mrs. Ramsay herself the role of one who possesses an entrance for Lily's desired penetration.

Such interdependence by which all supposed primacies—immediacy, authority, femininity—are a product of exchange rather than of essences is a clear part, then, of the Bloomsbury design of replacing modernist ideals in all their registers with the real structures of desire that produce them as ideological defenses. To be sure, we may for a moment consider the argument that the contamination of masculine and feminine tropes in the representation of Mrs. Ramsay's authority is a clue to her status as a phallic mother not unlike Molly Bloom. Like Mrs. Wilcox, she is a bearer of patriarchal law perhaps even sterner than that born(e) by the father himself, and therefore no more an exemplar of an essential femininity than anyone else in the novel. We may also consider the possibility that the figural contaminations are also in the service of an underlying notion of all power or authority as masculine in its social representation in an ineluctably patriarchal ideology (hence "kings," for example, is not a slip but an inevitability).

What remains clear in any case is that Tansley need not drop his innumerable tomes upon the floor in order to impress Mrs. Ramsay with the weight of his erudition. Like everything else in Bloomsbury, knowledge or power is not a thing but a relation. It is, of course, the power of relations—or the relations that constitute power—that *To the Lighthouse* as a text dynamizes as well as thematizes. The power of the text lies in the overt mobility of its structure, allowing Mrs. Ramsay's presence in part 1 to be a retroactive function of her absence in part 3 if one reads the novel in the reverse sequence it suggestively recommends as a metacritical commentary rather than as a mere eruption of the will to modernity itself. Long recognized as a paradigm for loss and belatedness thematically, the elegiac *To the Lighthouse* is also a formal paradigm for the problematic of modernism as a whole. Temporality is not just an issue but an active part of its mechanism and effect, requiring a double mode of reception by which the book may produce the presence of its referents while simultaneously demonstrating their absent and only deferred emergence within a purely discursive or semiotic field.

Chronology

1882	Adeline Virginia Stephen born in London on January 25 to Leslie Stephen, statesman and man of letters, and Julia Duckworth Stephen. Her father had one (insane) daughter from a previous marriage, her mother three children from an earlier marriage; together they had four more children: Vanessa, Julian Thoby, Virginia, and Adrian. Virginia educated at home by her parents.
1895	Julia Stephen dies; Leslie Stephen goes into deep mourning; Virginia has a severe mental breakdown. Household run by Julia's daughter Stella Duckworth, who postpones her marriage until Vanessa is old enough to take over.
1897	Stella Duckworth marries, becomes pregnant, and dies.
1902	Leslie Stephen knighted.
1904–5	Death of Sir Leslie Stephen in 1904. Virginia has a second mental breakdown and attempts suicide by jumping out of a window. Vanessa, Thoby, Virginia, and Adrian move to the Bloomsbury section of London. Virginia publishes first essays; soon becomes a regular book reviewer for the *Times Literary Supplement.* She also teaches at an evening college for working men and women.
1906	The four Stephens travel to Greece, where Vanessa and Thoby become ill; Thoby dies of typhoid fever at the age of 26.
1907	Vanessa Stephen marries artist Clive Bell; Virginia and Adrian share a flat near the Bells.
1910	First Postimpressionist Exhibition, engineered by Virginia's friend, critic Roger Fry. Gradual gathering of "Bloomsbury Group," comprising such people as Lytton Strachey, Roger Fry, Duncan Grant, Desmond MacCarthy, John Maynard Keynes and E. M. Forster.
1912–15	Virginia Stephen marries Leonard Woolf on August 10, 1912. She has third mental breakdown, which lasts for three years.

	During this time she completes novel, *The Voyage Out* (originally titled *Melymbrosia*), but its publication is delayed by her breakdown and by the beginning of World War I in 1914. Finally published in 1915 by her half-brother, Gerald Duckworth. Woolf begins diary.
1917	The Woolfs buy a secondhand printing press and set up the Hogarth Press, later to publish Forster, Dostoevsky, T. S. Eliot, Katherine Mansfield, Freud, Gorki, and Woolf's novels and writings.
1919	The novel *Night and Day*, and collections of short stories published.
1921	*Monday or Tuesday*, short fiction, published.
1922	*Jacob's Room.*
1925	*Mrs. Dalloway*; *The Common Reader*, a collection of essays. The Hogarth Press moves from the Woolfs' basement in Richmond to London.
1927	*To the Lighthouse.*
1928	*Orlando.*
1929	Book-length, feminist essay, *A Room of One's Own.*
1931	*The Waves.*
1932	*The Common Reader: Second Series.*
1933	*Flush*, a "biography" of Elizabeth Barrett Browning's spaniel.
1935	Virginia Woolf produces *Freshwater, A Comedy in Three Acts*, for her friends.
1937	Publishes *The Years.*
1938	*Three Guineas*, a pacifist, feminist essay.
1939	War declared on September 3; the Woolfs prepared to commit suicide if England invaded.
1940	*Roger Fry: A Biography.* Completes draft of *Between the Acts.* During Battle of Britain, London home destroyed by bombs.
1941	At the onset of another mental breakdown, which she fears will be permanent, Virginia Woolf drowns herself in the River Ouse on March 28, leaving suicide notes for her husband and sister. Leonard Woolf subsequently publishes various essays, short stories, letters, and diaries of hers, as well as several autobiographies which detail their life together.
1969	Leonard Woolf dies.

Contributors

HAROLD BLOOM, Sterling Professor of the Humanities at Yale University, is the author of *The Anxiety of Influence*, *Poetry and Repression*, and many other volumes of literary criticism. His forthcoming study, *Freud: Transference and Authority*, attempts a full-scale reading of all of Freud's major writings. A MacArthur Prize Fellow, he is general editor of five series of literary criticism published by Chelsea House. During 1987–88, he served as Charles Eliot Norton Professor of Poetry at Harvard.

HERMIONE LEE is a Lecturer in English at York University. In addition to regular reviews of fiction for *The Observer* and *The Times Literary Supplement*, her critical studies include *The Novels of Virginia Woolf*, *Elizabeth Bowen: An Estimation*, and *Philip Roth*. Her most recent work is a selection from the writings of Stevie Smith.

JANE LILIENFELD teaches English and Women's Studies at Assumption College and is the author of essays on Virginia Woolf and Margaret Atwood.

JOHN BURT is Assistant Professor of English at Brandeis University. His essay on *World Enough and Time* is included in *Robert Penn Warren: Modern Critical Views*.

GILLIAN BEER is a University Lecturer in English and Fellow of Girton College, Cambridge. She has published widely on nineteenth-century fiction. Her latest book is *Darwin's Plots: Evolutionary Narrative in Darwin, George Eliot and Nineteenth-Century Fiction*.

FRANK GLOVERSMITH was a tutor at Queens' College, Cambridge, and has taught in the United States and in Germany. He has edited Elizabeth Gaskell's *Wives and Daughters*, as well as writing on D. H. Lawrence's *The Rainbow* and editing *Class Culture and Social Change: A New View of the 1930s*.

BERNARD BERGONZI has been Professor of English at Warwick University since 1971. He is the author of several books on modern literature, including *The Situation of the Novel* and *Reading the Thirties*. He has also published a novel, *The Roman Persuasion*.

JOHN HARVEY is a University Lecturer in English and Fellow of Emmanuel College, Cambridge. His critical writings include a study of Victorian novelists and their illustrators. His novel, *The Plate Shop*, was awarded the David Higham Prize for fiction. He has recently completed a second novel on Greek politics.

IRIS MURDOCH, formerly lecturer in philosophy at St. Anne's College, Oxford, has published critical studies of Sartre and Plato. She is one of the most distinguished and prolific novelists in England today, her most recent novel being *The Good Apprentice*.

PERRY MEISEL is Professor of English at New York University. His books include *Thomas Hardy: The Return of the Repressed*, *The Absent Father: Virginia Woolf and Walter Pater*, and, with Walter Kendrick as coeditor, *Bloomsbury/Freud: The Letters of James and Alix Strachey*.

Bibliography

Adams, Kate. "Root and Branch: Mrs. Ramsay and Lily Briscoe in *To the Lighthouse*." *San Jose Studies* 9, no. 2 (1983): 93–109.

Albright, Daniel. *Personality and Impersonality: Lawrence, Woolf, and Mann*. Chicago: University of Chicago Press, 1978.

Apter, T. E. *Virginia Woolf: A Study of Her Novels*. New York: New York University Press, 1979.

Auerbach, Erich. "The Bown Stocking." In *Mimesis: The Representation of Reality in Western Literature*. Translated by W. R. Trask. Princeton: Princeton University Press, 1953.

Bassoff, Bruce. "Tables in Trees: Realism in *To the Lighthouse*." *Studies in the Novel* 16 (1984): 424–34.

Beer, Gillian. "Beyond Determinism: George Eliot and Virginia Woolf." In *Women Writing and Writing about Women*, edited by M. Jacobus. London: Croom Helm, 1979.

Béjà, Morris. "Virginia Woolf: Matches Struck in the Dark." in *Epiphany in the Modern Novel*. London: Peter Owen, 1971.

——, ed. *Virginia Woolf:* To the Lighthouse. London: Macmillan, 1970.

Bennett, Joan. *Virginia Woolf: Her Art as a Novelist*. New York: Harcourt Brace, 1945.

Blanchot, Maurice. "Outwitting the Demon—a Vocation." In *The Sirens' Song*, translated by Sacha Rabinovitch. Bloomington: Indiana University Press, 1982.

Brower, R. A. *The Fields of Light: An Experiment in Critical Reading*. New York: Oxford University Press, 1951.

Brown, Edward Killoran. *Rhythm in the Novel*. Toronto: Toronto University Press, 1949.

Burling, William J. "Virginia Woolf's 'Lighthouse': An Allusion to Shelley's *Queen Mab*?" *English Language Notes* 22 (December 1984): 62–65.

Clements, Patricia, and Isobel Grundy, eds. *Virginia Woolf: New Critical Essays*. Totowa, N. J.: Barnes & Noble, 1983.

Corsa, Helen Storm. "Death, Mourning, and Transfiguration in *To the Lighthouse*." *Literature and Psychology* 21 (3 November 1971): 120–22.

Di Battista, Maria. *Virginia Woolf's Major Novels: The Fables of Anon*. New Haven: Yale University Press, 1980.

Dick, Susan. "The Restless Searcher: A Discussion of the Evolution of 'Time Passes' in *To the Lighthouse*." *English Studies in Canada* 5 (1979): 311–29.

Fleishman, Avrom. *Virginia Woolf: A Critical Reading*. Baltimore: The Johns Hopkins University Press, 1975.

———. "Woolf and McTaggart." In *Fiction and the Ways of Knowing*, 163–78. Austin: University of Texas Press, 1978.

Freedman, Ralph, ed. *Virginia Woolf: Revaluation and Continuity.* Berkeley and Los Angeles: University of California Press, 1980.

Ginsberg, Elaine K., and Laura Moss Gottlieb, eds. *Virginia Woolf: Centennial Essays.* Troy, N.Y.: Whitston, 1983.

Gordon, Lyndall. *Virginia Woolf, A Writer's Life.* Oxford: Oxford University Press, 1984.

Guth, Deborah. "Virginia Woolf: Myth and *To the Lighthouse.*" *College Literature* 11 (1984): 233–49.

Harrington, Harry R. "The Central Line Down the Middle of *To the Lighthouse.*" *Contemporary Literature* 21 (1980): 363–83.

Hartman, Geoffrey H. *Beyond Formalism: Literary Essays 1958–1970.* New Haven: Yale University Press, 1970.

Heilbrun, Carolyn G. "The Bloomsbury Group." In *Toward a Recognition of Androgyny*, 113–67. New York: Alfred A. Knopf, 1973.

Hoffman, Anne Golomb. "Demeter and Poseidon: Fusion and Distance in *To the Lighthouse.*" *Studies in the Novel* 16 (1984): 182–96.

Hussey, Mark. *The Singing of the Real World: The Philosophy of Virginia Woolf's Fiction.* Columbus: Ohio State University Press, 1986.

Kapur, Vijay. *Virginia Woolf's Vision of Life and Her Search for Significant Form: A Study in the Shaping Vision.* Atlantic Highlands, N.J.: Humanities Press, 1981.

Kiely, Robert. *Beyond Egotism: The Fiction of James Joyce, Virginia Woolf and D. H. Lawrence.* Cambridge: Harvard University Press, 1980.

Leaska, Mitchell. *Virginia Woolf's Lighthouse.* New York: Columbia University Press, 1971.

Lewis, Thomas S. W. *Virginia Woolf.* New York: McGraw-Hill, 1975.

Little, Judy. *Comedy and the Woman Writer: Woolf, Spark, and Feminism.* Lincoln: University of Nebraska Press, 1983.

Lodge, David. *The Modes of Modern Writing.* London: E. Arnold, 1977.

McCluskey, Kathleen, C. S. J. *Reverberations: Sound and Structure in the Novels of Virginia Woolf.* Ann Arbor: UMI Research Press, 1986.

McLaurin, Allen. *Virginia Woolf: The Echoes Enslaved.* Cambridge: Cambridge University Press, 1973.

Marcus, Jane, ed. *New Feminist Essays on Virginia Woolf.* Lincoln: University of Nebraska Press, 1981.

———, ed. *Virginia Woolf: A New Feminist Slant.* Lincoln: University of Nebraska Press, 1983.

Marder, Herbert. *Feminism and Art: A Study of Virginia Woolf.* Chicago: University of Chicago Press, 1968.

Matro, Thomas G. "Only Relations: Vision and Achievement in *To the Lighthouse.*" *PMLA* 99 (1984): 212–24.

May, Keith M., "The Symbol of Painting in Virginia Woolf's *To the Lighthouse.*" *Review of English Literature* 8 (April 1967): 91–98.

Meisel, Perry. "The Common Life." In *The Absent Father: Virginia Woolf and Walter Pater.* New Haven: Yale University Press, 1980.

Mepham, John. "Figures of Desire: Narration and Fiction in *To the Lighthouse.*" In *The Modern English Novel,* edited by G. Josipovici, 149–85. London: Open Books, 1976.

Miller, J. Hillis. "Mr. Carmichael and Lily Briscoe: The Rhythm and Creativity in *To the Lighthouse.*" In *Modernism Reconsidered*, edited by Robert Kiely. Cambridge: Harvard University Press, 1983.

Naremore, James. *The World Without a Self: Virginia Woolf and the Novel.* New Haven: Yale University Press, 1973.

Parkes, Graham. "Imagining Reality in *To the Lighthouse.*" *Philosophy and Literature* 6 (1982): 33–44.

Paterson, John. *The Novel as Faith: The Gospel According to James, Hardy, Conrad, Joyce, Lawrence and Virginia Woolf.* Boston: Gambit, 1973.

Poresky, Louise A. *The Elusive Self: Psyche and Spirit in Virginia Woolf's Novels.* Newark: University of Delaware Press, 1981.

Ragussis, Michael. *Acts of Naming: the Family Plot in Fiction.* New York: Oxford University Press, 1986.

Ruddick, Lisa. *The Seen and the Unseen: Virginia Woolf's* To the Lighthouse. Cambridge: Harvard University Press, 1977.

Sarraute, Nathalie. "Conversation and Sub-Conversation." In *Tropisms and The Age of Suspicion*, translated by Maria Jolas. London: John Calder, 1963.

Schaefer, Josephine O'Brien. *The Threefold Nature of Reality in the Novels of Virginia Woolf.* The Hague: Mouton, 1965.

Showalter, Elaine, ed. *The New Feminist Criticism: Essays on Women, Literature and Theory.* New York: Pantheon, 1985.

Spilka, Mark. "On Lily Briscoe's Borrowed Grief: A Psycho-Literary Speculation." *Criticism* 21 (1979): 1–33.

Spivak, Gayatri C. "Unmaking and Making in *To the Lighthouse.*" In *Women and Language in Literature and Society*, edited by Sally McConell-Ginet, Ruth Borker, and Nelly Furman, 310–27. New York: Praeger, 1980.

Stewart, Garett. *Death Sentences: Styles of Dying in British Fiction.* Cambridge: Harvard University Press, 1984.

Stewart, Jack F. "Impressionism in the Early Novels of Virginia Woolf." *Journal of Modern Literature* 9 (1982): 237–66.

———. "Light in *To the Lighthouse.*" *Twentieth Century Literature* 23 (1977): 377–89.

Tindall, W. Y. *The Literary Symbol.* Bloomington: Indiana University Press, 1955.

Torgovnick, Marianna. *The Visual Arts, Pictorialism, and the Novel: James, Lawrence, and Woolf.* Princeton: Princeton University Press, 1985.

Virginia Woolf Quarterly, 1972–.

Vogler, Thomas A., ed. *Twentieth Century Interpretations of* To the Lighthouse: *A Collection of Critical Essays.* Englewood Cliffs, N.J.: Prentice-Hall, 1970.

Wyatt, Jean. "The Celebrations of Eros: Greek Concepts of Love and Beauty in *To the Lighthouse.*" *Philosophy and Literature* 2 (1978): 160–75.

Acknowledgments

"*To the Lighthouse:* Completed Forms" (originally entitled "*To the Lighthouse*, 1927") by Hermione Lee from *The Novels of Virginia Woolf* by Hermione Lee, © 1977 by Hermione Lee. Reprinted by permission of Methuen & Co. Ltd.

" 'The Deceptiveness of Beauty': Mother Love and Mother Hate in *To the Lighthouse*" by Jane Lilienfeld from *Twentieth-Century Literature* 23, no. 3 (October 1977), © 1977 by Hofstra University Press. Reprinted by permission.

"Mysticism and Atheism in *To the Lighthouse*" by Martin Corner from *Studies in the Novel* 13, no. 4 (Winter 1981), © 1981 by North Texas State University. Reprinted by permission.

"Irreconcilable Habits of Thought in *A Room of One's Own* and *To the Lighthouse*" by John Burt from *ELH* 49, no. 4 (Winter 1982), © 1982 by the Johns Hopkins University Press, Baltimore/London. Reprinted by permission of the Johns Hopkins University Press.

"Hume, Stephen, and Elegy in *To the Lighthouse*" by Gillian Beer from *Essays in Criticism* 34, no. 1 (January 1984), © 1984 by Stephen Wall. Reprinted by permission of the Editors of *Essays in Criticism*.

"Autonomy Theory" (originally entitled "Autonomy Theory: Ortega, Roger Fry, Virginia Woolf") by Frank Gloversmith from *The Theory of Reading*, edited by Frank Gloversmith, © 1984 by Frank Gloversmith. Reprinted by permission of Barnes & Noble Books, Totowa, New Jersey, and The Harvester Press Ltd.

"Panel Discussion" (originally entitled "Panel Discussion I") by Gillian Beer (Chair), Bernard Bergonzi, John Harvey, and Iris Murdoch from *Virginia Woolf, a Centenary Perspective*, edited by Eric Warner, © 1984 by Eric Warner. Reprinted by permission of the Macmillan Press and St. Martin's Press, Inc.

"Deferred Action in *To the Lighthouse*" by Perry Meisel from *The Myth of the Modern: A Study in British Literature and Criticism after 1850* by Perry Meisel, © 1987 by Yale University. Reprinted by permission of Yale University Press.

Index